The Ba

Handbook

A step-by-step guide to buying a barge

DBA – The Barge Association 2022

Contents

Researched, written & published by
The Dutch Barge Association Ltd
Cormorant, Spade Oak Reach, Cookham SL6 9RQ
Phone 0044 (0) 303 666 0636
Website www.barges.org
E-mail info@barges.org
2022 The Barge Buyer's Handbook Seventh edition
Printed and bound on demand in Great Britain by Cambrian Press

This handbook has been produced by the joint efforts of DBA members. Our grateful thanks go to everyone who has contributed to the creation of the book, for writing and proof reading, for additional material and corrections, for photographs and illustrations, for design and production.

Profits from the sale of the handbook go to the DBA and help to support the work of the Association.

Andy Soper
Vice-Chairman
February 2022

Changes and mistakes

We have done our best to ensure that all the information in this book is correct. However, as we deal with hundreds of details, it is possible that an error has occasionally slipped in. Do please let us know of any errors you notice. As every reasonable care has been taken in the preparation of this book, we can accept no responsibility for errors, omissions, or damage, however caused.

ISBN 978-1-7397437-0-3

PREFACE TO THE SEVENTH EDITION

We discovered the second edition of this book shortly after we decided that a life afloat was our next move. It proved to be invaluable to me, a seagoing marine engineer, as a guide to the intricacies of finding, choosing and understanding Dutch barges – so different from our UK canal narrowboats. It was also a valuable asset in reassuring my wife that others had gone this way and found success!

This handbook, written by our members, has just undergone a major revision. It is to the credit of the original authors that nearly all of their advice is still valid today! We have updated telephone numbers, e-mail addresses, and costs. Inevitably legislation has increased and become more complicated, especially post BREXIT, and technology has moved on and we have tried to reflect all of that in the content. On these and some other fast-moving issues we have referred you to the DBA website barges.org for more information – but you may need to join to get the full picture.

I often hear the refrain 'we are looking for a barge and we'll join the DBA when we have one'. If you are thinking of buying a barge you need this book and membership now!

My thanks to Tim Cadle, Chris Grant, Stan and Sharon Hammond, Hilary Pereira and Caroline Soper for their help in producing this revised edition – but all the errors are mine!

Andy Soper
Vice-Chairman
DBA – The Barge Association
db Neeltje
Cookham

INTRODUCTION

Many people have found buying barges difficult. Most buyers have learned a lot from the venture, particularly from first purchases, and would do it better or at least differently another time. We felt it worthwhile to try to give you the chance of avoiding some pitfalls by letting you benefit from the combined experience of your predecessors.

We have been able to collect this experience largely because of our Association, which attracted the many contributors to this book. The Association's aims are to bring together barge enthusiasts, to work with other organisations with compatible aims, and to communicate on behalf of our members with navigation authorities and other official bodies. Many members own barges, others are dreaming of doing so, some are 'just looking'.

The Association was formed because of a need for an organisation for those interested in the sort of craft not always welcome at the yacht club. While its name is 'DBA - The Barge Association', it welcomes those interested in any type of barge (or indeed any inland craft). It matters not whether the vessel is a Humber keel, narrowboat, Leeds & Liverpool short boat, Polish tug, German torpedo recovery launch, or luxemotor.

We make representations to authorities on matters such as maintenance of waterways for barge traffic, navigation charges, and barge 'driver's licences'. We organise rallies regularly, both in England and elsewhere. We have a growing number of contacts with businesses involved with barges in a commercial or professional capacity, very useful for sourcing equipment peculiar to barges and for advice and discounts. We also publish a magazine, Blue Flag, which contains useful technical and other factual information for present and potential barge owners, and relays interesting and amusing experiences to give members some of the feeling of what barging is all about.

This will sound like an advertisement, which it is, but it also leads to the first serious piece of advice to the prospective barge owner. Join us. You are almost bound to find support and help available through the Association to be very valuable. If nothing else, it will introduce you to people sympathetic to your problems.

So welcome to our Barge Buyer's Handbook. We hope you find it useful, whether you are buying a barge or already own one. However, a couple of provisos: this handbook contains the work of a number of people who inevitably have some differences of opinion, so contrasting views have been included where they suggest a range of sensible choices.

While reasonable efforts have been made to ensure the accuracy and appropriateness of the handbook, the Association cannot take responsibility for its contents or for omissions. Always try to confirm the information for yourself.

SUMMARY OF CONTENTS

This handbook is organised into chapters to match the topics most people have to deal with as they approach barge ownership. This may be a logical order, but it will not necessarily be the sequence you follow. Barge buying is not that tidy.

1 It starts with answers to the question you will almost certainly be asked early in the game: 'Have you taken leave of your senses?'.

2 You soon discover how varied barges are. What should yours be like? We take you through the crucial process of deciding what you are looking for, and help you decide what characteristics you want your barge to have.

3 Only when you have a picture of the barge you are after can you decide whether you can afford it. No, not the purchase price (that comes in a following chapter). Here we take you through the real expense: the costs of owning a barge.

4 In case we have not frightened you off yet, we go on to describe the market for barges. What can you expect to find for sale, and at what prices?

5 Some barges used for pleasure are over 50 years old, so condition is a vital consideration. We make suggestions as to what you should look for during your first viewing, introduce the all-important survey, and discuss the various other documents you should expect to see.

6 Your search can then begin in earnest. We cover where to look, and how to work with brokers.

7 Because you may end up buying your barge in another country, we take you through the purchase transaction in some detail including the taxation changes introduced by UK leaving the EU. This includes how to negotiate the contract, what commitments the parties are making, what paperwork is needed, and details of the survey.

8 Finally, when you have bought your barge, then what? We end with some ideas on getting it home, particularly if you have never steered anything larger than a dinghy or a narrowboat before.
We include in the Appendices, a bibliography, a checklist to help you through the process, and a list of contacts you may find useful.

Don't worry if this all sounds daunting. Thousands of people have gone through the process successfully, and there is no reason why you should not do so too. But do be prepared for a few experiences which may later result in amusing stories in the bar (or the wheelhouse).

YOU WANT TO BUY A WHAT?

Although your acquaintances may not think so, there are several very sensible reasons for owning a barge:

- It can be one of the most comfortable and manageable craft for cruising.
- It can make a commodious and unique home.
- It can be an absorbing interest, with a fascinating sense of history. And, in all these aspects, it can be surprisingly cost-effective.

Of course, there are also some negative points. We will get to them too.

CRUISING

We assume you are already aware of the delights of the inland waterways. However, if you are familiar only with routes in the UK, you have the enormous joys of the huge mainland Europe network to come.

A major advantage of a barge for inland cruising is that you get a lot for your money. The vessel is likely to have much more space afloat than anything else most of us could conceivably afford. Moreover, since weight of goods on board is not a problem, a barge can readily include all mod. cons. (a typical barge can carry at least 50T; you are unlikely to have more than 5T of domestic possessions). It can literally be a home away from home.

Barges are tough. They were designed to take the knocks of inland freight carrying, so they can easily take pleasure travel in their stride. If you have navigated in a conventional pleasure boat, you will find the lack of worry with a barge about occasional grounding or glancing contact with navigation works a great relief. If damage does occur, repairs to steel work are usually less costly than equivalent work on a fibreglass or wooden craft.

Barges are much easier to handle than you might expect. Why this is so becomes clear when you think about their history. Barges are, or were, business tools, devices for carrying freight at a profit. They were designed and evolved to do this efficiently, which meant not only having as much room inside as possible for their size (for freight) and being able to move through the water while consuming as little fuel as possible, but also being able to be run by as few crew as possible. This has resulted in the right equipment being incorporated, carefully designed and located to do the jobs needed with minimum effort. The outcome is that most of the types of barge we are interested in can be navigated readily by two people, and can even be moved successfully by one person at a pinch.

RESIDENCE

The shape of most barges allows them to become a convenient and space-efficient residence. They are very stable on inland waters (which means, among other things, they do not tip when you step on board), and most can safely take the ground on a drying tidal mooring.
It is not all rosy, of course.

Mortgages for barges are less readily available and usually attract higher interest rates than those for houses. Also, finding any acceptable residential mooring, let alone a charming one with secure tenure, can be a significant problem, especially in Britain. A barge can be as cosy as a modern house, but a badly converted one can be damp and chilly.

Many people have found that once they have lived on a barge they cannot imagine why they ever had a house or flat. There is something very special about having a barge for a home, despite the occasional hassle.

HERITAGE

At boat shows you can sometimes see newly built barges on sale. They are certainly a good option and for many purchasers, are the ideal answer. A (sometimes hefty) premium can be well worth it for the peace of mind of a new hull and new equipment. A new barge can be less expensive than buying, converting and renovating an older one. New-builds vary considerably in design and quality. Some are excellent. Few, though, are exact copies of the original. Many have much simpler shapes (above and below the waterline), which can affect aesthetics and handling. And of course, though they have their own character, they won't have that heritage feeling.

Many buyers choose ex-working vessels. Few of these were built after the 1930s in the popular sizes and some are over one hundred years old. Yes, this raises immediate worries about maintenance and condition, but it also gives the craft very special and individual character and interest. The barge vendor will often be able to tell you, usually with some pride, about the vessel's history – where it worked, what it carried, who its crew were, what unusual things happened to it. It can feel good to know that your barge used to take tulips to the flower market, or even stront (the Dutch word for a certain natural product) out to fertilise the fields.

As with all antiques, the design and construction of barges varies widely, and there is much debate about which features are most useful, clever, or beautiful. The subtle (or not so subtle) marks of an honourable working life can give today's owner the warm feeling of a link with earlier days.

You may decide to look for a barge with particular historic features, or keep or change those your vessel happens to come with. For instance, is the single-cylinder engine which you have to start with a blow lamp your idea of owning a piece of industrial archaeology, or will you replace it instantly with a modern diesel?

WHAT CHARACTERISTICS SHOULD YOUR BARGE HAVE?

Most freight barges were designed for specific traffics and routes. With a whole continent of extensive inland waterways, it is not surprising that they vary enormously. Although this choice may seem overwhelming at first, it is actually an advantage as it gives you, the buyer the chance to find exactly what you want.

The key initial question is probably size: we explore this topic in some detail below. Aesthetics must also be heeded, so we cover the various styles; also 'motor vs sailing'. We end this section with considerations of the quality of the conversion and accommodation, and some thoughts on doing your own conversion or update.

EFFECTS OF SIZE

Barges come in many sizes. Although it may be possible to change any of a barge's dimensions (more on this below), it is a lot cheaper not to. Getting one that is already the size you want is definitely a good idea. But what is that size? Answering this question is something you should spend considerable time on before buying.

Size is a major determinant of cruising range, accommodation, costs of ownership (mooring and maintenance in particular), availability of moorings, availability of dry docks, and regulations. Perhaps surprisingly though, the purchase price does not necessarily grow with the barge because above a certain size barges get less desirable for leisure use.

CRUISING RANGE

The main consideration limiting your choice of size may be where you want to go with your barge. The bigger the vessel, the fewer inland routes it will fit. Be realistic. You may never brave the potentially treacherous Irish Sea with a craft designed for quiet inland waters, so why limit your vessel's length to that of the locks on the Grand Canal between Dublin and the Shannon? Or not go as far South as the Canal du Midi with its restricting Capestang bridge. One member responded to the question as to why his barge was too large for Capestang – 'It fits 10,000 km of European waterways – probably enough for me'!

Navigation gauges vary as much as barge sizes. Although many waterways were built to one of several 'standard' gauges, there were a lot of local initiatives too, so it is hard to generalise. The best approach may be to familiarise yourself with the waterways map (see Appendix II) and with waterway dimensions for your hoped-for cruising range, and then to decide which routes you are prepared to forego if you want a bigger vessel.

We include a table of waterway gauges, but with important reservations. The table (p. 21) gives maximum length and beam (width) for most routes listed, and you can usually approach these limits with some confidence.

You also need to consider draft (the depth of the water) and air draft (the clearance above the water). For these dimensions, more caution is advised. It is too easy to get stuck in poorly dredged or rubbish-filled channels where water levels are low, or under low, especially arched, bridges when water levels are high. In practice, you will be glad later that you allowed a generous clearance above and below.

Officially quoted waterway dimensions can be misleading. Fortunately, they tend more often to be conservative than optimistic, except in the all too frequent cases of dredging arrears. Sometimes the actual gauge is surprisingly larger than the official one, especially in Britain. There are some counter-examples, though: in the UK some bridges are reinforced with sprayed concrete, which has reduced the width to below the official dimension, or (on arched bridges) the width at which the official air draft applies. If a dimension is crucial, ask around and get opinions based on recent local experience.

Air draft is probably the most awkward dimension. It is significantly affected by bridge and vessel shapes, and is virtually impossible to specify accurately for many routes given the variations in bridge design.

The only sure solution is to seek informed local knowledge and to measure key bridges yourself. To do this, identify both the lowest flat bridge and any notoriously tight arched ones. An arched bridge can be checked quite easily by measuring the headroom every 30cm or so across the bridge hole with a plumb line. Do not forget to note whether the water is up to its normal level. If the towpath passes under the bridge, record how far it sticks out. A minimum bridge cross-section can then be drawn and compared with a scale drawing of your intended vessel's cross-section.

You may wish to cruise in the British Isles as well as in mainland Europe, so the table covers principal waterways there. It excludes the extensive network of English narrow boat canals, which only accepts craft up to 2.1m wide. It does include some barge navigations which are derelict at present but which may return to life while you are a barge owner.

British barge waterways are both varied and small in European terms. They have developed little since they were originally built. UK waterway dimensions generally decrease as you move inland from tidal waters. For example, although the locks on the River Medway are all about the same size, the navigation channel is about 2m deep at Maidstone but only 1.2m deep at the head of navigation at Tonbridge. On the Thames, locks tend to be smaller further upstream. For example, Shepperton Lock (near London) measures 53.1m x 6.0m, while St Johns Lock, near the head of navigation at Lechlade, is only 33.6m x 4.5m. Bridge headrooms also become less generous further upstream. The maximum comfortable draft is not much over 1m if you want to venture off main rivers, and 0.9m is better. Even on such routes as the Thames, exceeding 1.2m may limit your range and pleasure. You will start to cut your cruising range seriously with an air draft of more than 2.1m (with the wheelhouse down), particularly if you have a wide superstructure at that height. The Kennet & Avon navigation, a major east–west route, cannot take any more than that, the Thames above Oxford not much more, and the arched bridges on the Grand Union Canal, a major north–south route, are definitely unpleasant for barges much taller.

At present, the UK barge navigations are divided into regional networks in the south, east and north connected by narrow canals which could be widened, derelict barge navigations which could be restored, or unnavigable rivers which could be opened. Several projects to create such links are at various stages of progress at the moment, so inland barge cruising from one end of the UK to the other may become a possibility one day.

The table (see page 21) includes the majority of the French waterways, but leaves out a number not connected to the main network and omits such narrow oddities as the Canal de l'Ourcq and the largely derelict Canal du Berry (although a project to restore at least part of this is now under way). If one foregoes access to the British rivers and 'wide' canals, the next effective size constraints are the dimensions of some routes in France which are smaller than the Freycinet dimensions. The (full) Freycinet dimensions are a standard introduced in the nineteenth century by a French minister of transport (Monsieur Freycinet, bien sûr), who set the following gauge for French waterways (dimensions in metres):

Length   38.5   Beam 5.05
Air draft 3.5   Draft 1.8

Most French and Belgian waterways were upgraded to this standard after the 1880s, and subsequently most barges using them were built to these maximum dimensions. But some waterways and some barges were not. A Freycinet-gauge barge is often called a 'péniche' in France or a 'spits' in the Low Countries.

Waterways isolated from the main network, such as those in Brittany, tended not to be rebuilt to the Freycinet standard. There were also some notable exclusions within the French network for various historic reasons, some of which you may well want to use. The principal ones are the Canal de Bourgogne, Canal du Midi, and Canal du Nivernais.

A fixed air draft of 3.5m will in theory allow travel almost anywhere in France – but sometimes only with great care. An air draft of 3.4m will give much greater peace of mind. A demountable wheelhouse reducing air draft to no more than 2.7m gives the most flexibility.

The table does not include waterways in the Netherlands, as routes of almost every size exist there, originally designed for vessels carrying from 5T through to over 24,000T, and often (and still being) upgraded. In general a Freycinet vessel will get to enough Dutch places to satisfy most people. However, check the sizes of the smaller canals if you hope to ditch-crawl up charming tiny routes. The standard reference work on them is the Almanak voor Watertoerisme, published by the ANWB, the Dutch tourist board. It is quite understandable to anglophones even though available only in Dutch (there are pages with translations for useful terms).

There are a number of computer programs that allow passage planning – originally developed for commercial craft – but invaluable for recreational cruising. The market leader is probably PC Navigo: (https://www.pcnavigo.com/?lang=en)
It always errs, dimensionally, on the safe side and you might creep through some bridges and locks. It is good for detailed information on stoppages, contact telephone numbers for locks and bridges, and daily planning.

ACCOMMODATION

It is an iron rule that no matter how large a vessel you buy, you will eventually wish it had more space inside. You will at various times want more berths, more storage, more room for equipment, or a squash court (not necessarily a joke – we know of one barge with a front-garden size lawn on the cabin top, and others with a swimming pool).
There is also the question of hold depth. Barges were built with differing sizes of hold to allow for such factors as the density of freight to be carried and the depths of waterways to be used. In the larger sizes, holds can seem vastly deep: two-storey (or deck, if you must) conversions are possible.

If one storey will do, a reasonably shallow hold is often more suitable. You are then likely to be able to see out of the windows while you are standing on the floor inside or even sitting at the dining table. It is true that this can be achieved in a deeper hold by building the floor well above the bottom of the vessel, but see further comments below on this technique. In a very deep hold, you may have to depend on skylights for light, and these can leak or drip condensation.

Freycinet-gauge barges are still available at the moment as they are becoming uneconomic for freight and many commercial owners are now retired and planning to move ashore, and the large volume of space they offer can be tempting. However, many people find they really do not need this much space, the holds are too deep, and a barge this big is just too much of a good thing. Commodious accommodation can be built into something considerably smaller.

Waterway Gauges

South Waterways Network	Length	Width	Draft	Air Draft	Locks	Miles	Comments
Avon, River (Stratford)	21m	4.1m	0.8m	3m	17	14	
Chelmer & Blackwater	18m	4.3m	0.8m	2m	13	14	Not connected to main network. Access via coast.
Gloucester & Sharpness	41.15m	6.4m	1.83m	7.5m	2	30	
Grand Union (London – Braunston)	21.95m	3.81m	1.1m	1.9m	102	109	
Grand Union (Braunston – Birmingham)	21.95m	3.81m	1.1m	1.9m	57	41	
Grand Union Canal (Slough Branch)	21.95m	4.92m	1.1m	2.33m	0	5	
Kennet & Avon Canal	21.95m	4m	0.9m	2.4m	106	96	
Lee, River	22.86m	4.72m	1.3m	2.11m	34	40	
Stort, River	26.8m	3.87m	1.1m	1.95m			
Medway (Allington Lock – Maidstone)	24m	6m	1.7m	3.7m	10	42	
Medway (Maidstone – Tonbridge)	24m	5.8m	1.2m	1.9m			
Regents Canal	22m	4.34m	1.17m	2.67m	11	21	Islington and Maida Hill tunnels reported 6ft 10ins air draft
Severn, River	27.m	5.7m	1.83m	6.1m	4	38	
Thames, River	40m	4.2m	0.9m	2.28m	44	168	Osney bridge limiting height
Wey & Godalming	21.95m	4.1m	0.9m	2m	16	20	
Basingstoke Canal	21.9m	4.1m	1m	2m	29	32	

North Waterways Network	Length	Width	Draft	Air Draft	Locks	Miles	Comments
Aire & Calder	61m	5.4m	2.3m	3.6m	17	42	
Bridgewater Canal	15.3m	3.2m	0.9m	2.1m	3	40	Preston Brook tunnel reported low
Calder & Hebble Navigation	17.5m	4.32m	1.07m	2.85m	39	21	
Fossdyke Canal & R Witham Nav (Torksey– Boston)	21.3m	4.64m	1.52m	3.43m	4	48	
Huddersfield Broad Canal	17.5m	4.22m	1.3m	2.5m	9	4	
Lancaster Canal	22m	4.3m	0.9m	2.5m	0	42	
Leeds & Liverpool Canal (incl branches)	18.9m	4.3m	1.15m	2.28m	91	140	Gannow & Foulridge tunnels reported low
Ouse, River Yorkshire	17.5m	4.66m	1.2m	5.94m	4	68	
Rochdale (Sowerby Bridge – Todmorden)	21.95m	4.14m	1.2m	1.83m	100	34	
Selby Canal	23.9m	5m	1.2m	2.44m	5	24	
Sheffield & South Yorkshire (Keadby – Sheffield)	18.75m	4.65m	1.4m	3.05m	28	49	
Shropshire Union (to Nantwich)	21.95m	2.95m	1.2m	2.44m	17	26	
Soar, River & Grand Union Leicester Section	21.95m	3.05m	1m	2.13m	42	43	
Trent, River	21.34m	4.27m	1.1m	2.44m	11	95	

North East Waterways Network Connected to the North Waterways Network via the Wash

	Length	Width	Draft	Air Draft	Locks	Miles	Comments
Middle Level; Navigation	24m	3.5m	1m	2.13m	2.13	80	
Nene, River	26m	4.6m	1.1m	1.9m	38	90	Northampton to the Wash
Ouse, River Great	17.5m	4.66m		5.94m	16	75	General dimensions
Welland & Glen	22.86m	4m	1m	1.8m	2	47	Off the Wash
Witham Navigable Drains (Boston)	22.86m	5.4m	1.52m	2.74m	-	-	

Other Waterways	Length	Width	Draft	Air Draft	Locks	Miles	Comments
Norfolk Broads Network	14m	3.8m	1.2 m		2	100	Bye-laws – exemptions available
Forth & Clyde & Union Canal (Scotland)	20.47m	5m	1.8m	3m	-	-	
Ireland Canals	18m	4m	-	-	100+	300+	
France							
Brittany Waterways	25m	4.6m					
Canal de Bourgogne	38m	5.01m	1.6m	3.4m			
Canal du Midi	30m	5.01m	1.6m	3m			
Canal du Nivernais	30m	5.01m	1.6m	2.8m			
Freycinet Standard Waterways	38m	5.01m	2m	3.4m			

We have mentioned demountable wheelhouses before. You can increase your cruising range with one, but you will soon be fed up with putting it up and down if you have to do it too often. Demounting is particularly disruptive if you use the wheelhouse as your (fully furnished) living room.

The overall layout of the accommodation is important. Some conversions keep the separation of fore-cabin, hold and wheelhouse, so you have to go outside to pass from one to the other. Think about the disadvantages of making that trip in winter or in rough water. Others have stairs from the wheelhouse straight down into the hold accommodation, and an internal door into the fore end.

HANDLING

Most barges handle well, due to their stability and large rudders. But the bigger the barge and the smaller the waterway, the more challenging the navigation. The skill needed increases rapidly as any one of a vessel's dimensions approaches a route's size limits. Also, a full-gauge barge (such as a Freycinet barge on a Freycinet waterway) will travel quite slowly because water must squeeze through the small gaps left between barge and masonry or silt. Having some clearance to spare can make life much easier.

Putting two storeys in a barge requires a lot of ballast if the cabin top is to fit under bridges. The now much heavier barge is correspondingly trickier to manoeuvre and also harder to stop. Its added momentum gives it much greater capability to do serious damage if it hits something it should not. It is also deeper so more likely to run aground. As a result, many feel the two-storey approach tends to result in a barge too ponderous for general pleasure cruising. Perhaps it is better to leave it to the hotel péniches.

Similar considerations apply to a single-storey craft with a deep hold. You may still need a lot of ballast to help the barge get a grip on the water when you are trying to stop or make a turn. The space under the floor can be used for tanks, spare furniture, wine cellar, etc. but nonetheless conventional wisdom gives preference to a shallow hold and a modest draft.

Finally, there is handling at sea to consider, especially if you plan to do anything more than a dash across the Channel. Some, but by no means all, larger Dutch barges were built for both inland and estuary work, and occasionally as seagoing craft. They have stronger frames and a more marine shape than their strictly inland counterparts. Spits, though, are seldom suitable for the sea, as they were usually designed for inland use only. Their shapes are bluff, their construction is light, their plating is thin. Some have been known to break in the middle when taken into the sort of rough water which can be found even in such inland bodies as the Ijsselmeer.

OWNERSHIP COSTS

We go into ownership costs in more detail later, but some thought should be given to them here. There is no getting around it. Owning a big barge costs more than owning a small one.

Mooring is a key consideration. Mooring costs vary with length, whether the space is purchased, leased or rented. You may not need a permanent mooring initially, or for some time. You can cruise through Belgium, the Netherlands and France for years, never staying in one place for more than a few days, and incur negligible mooring charges along the way. However, in the end, most owners decide they want a base and the feeling of security it can bring.

Bigger boats cost more to maintain. Think of all the extra painting! Slips and dry docks tend to charge by the metre length, and surveyors by their time (they can test the thickness of only so many square metres of bottom in an hour).

Most navigation authorities levy charges (licences, vignettes) which vary with length, some even with multiples of dimensions, e.g. length x beam. Our Association considers this unfair, as few of the authorities' costs vary with craft size, but getting them to abandon this practice is proving a difficult battle.

REGULATIONS AND QUALIFICATIONS

Most nations consider a barge above a certain size to be a ship, and start applying ship-like regulations. These can include onerous registration and safety equipment provisions, and requirements that the skippers (and crew, when at sea) must have professional credentials. Generally barge skippers on barges below 24m will find the International Certificate of Competence (ICC) acceptable in most countries.

Currently you are not required to have any formal qualification to navigate a recreational craft in UK waters. However, we would urge you to gain an appropriate qualification through the RYA (Royal Yachting Association) training schemes. The Day Skipper qualification will ensure that you have gained the essential basic skills of seamanship and navigation.

If you plan to navigate in mainland Europe you will need the International Certificate of Competence (ICC) with a CEVNI (the European waterways code and signals) endorsement. Both of these can be gained through the RYA training schools. The ICC syllabus is similar to the Day Skipper qualification and the CEVNI test is multiple-choice test paper on aspects of the code.

Barges over 20m in length operating in mainland Europe are required to carry two VHF radios which must have the appropriate frequencies and the ability to transmit a special ATIS code. You will need a Short Range Operators Certificate qualifying you to use a VHF radio which can again be gained through the RYA.

There are European regulations for construction of all barges over 20m in length and an out of water survey is required every 7 years depending on country (Except in UK where the Boat Safety Scheme applies – in water safety checks every four years). This is the European Certificate – European Standard - Technical Regulations for Inland Navigation vessels (ES-TRIN) (previously TRIWV or CBB). All new craft, over 2.5m, built since 1998 have to comply with a further EU Directive – the Recreational Craft Directive (RCD) – see Chapter 6.

The web-site Knowledge Base, in the members' area of www.barges.org contains the most up to date information on all of these regulations and some information on how to interact with those regulations if you are not a UK or EU citizen.

In mainland Europe, the regulations vary from country to country and although intended to be common, do have local variations depending on the nationality of the vessel, how long you intend to stay in the country and the nationality of the skipper. It is usually more complex if the skipper is not an EU national.

If your situation is not clear cut, please contact the DBA by e-mail (info@barges.org) or telephone and we will give you up-to-date information.

CHANGING THE SIZE

What if you just cannot find a barge of the exact size you want? It happens, particularly if your search time is unavoidably short. You could consider changing one or more dimensions of a barge which is the wrong size.

Many barges were lengthened in the past to increase capacity, and these can be good prospects for shortening since this may restore the proportions and curves lost in the lengthening process. Some barges shorten well anyway, as they have uniform cross sections over a considerable length. At least one spits was very successfully shortened from 38m to 24m, leaving just the original forward and after accommodation, the engine room, and a small hold between for a workshop. However, do not forget that shortening does not reduce air draft or the depth of the hold, so not all short-comings of a large vessel can be dealt with in this way.

Similarly, a barge with a relatively constant cross-section can often be lengthened without much difficulty. This is more expensive than shortening, as a new section must be built. If you do opt for lengthening, it may be best to have the work done in the Netherlands. Yards there are used to this type of work, while managers of those in the UK tend to start muttering and multiplying cost estimates by large factors when you suggest such a project.

One DBA member's barge started its career a bit longer (and was shortened) and a bit wider (and was narrowed by pruning its wide rubbing bands) than he wanted. It was also too high, necessitating removal of the fixed wheelhouse and substitution of a demountable one, and too deep, so some ballast had to come out. The necessary surgery rendered it just the size he was after, but soon after it was done the owner saw a beautiful vessel for sale with exactly the right dimensions!

So are you after a clog-sized tjalk, or a Freycinet gauge spits? Make up your mind before you start looking. Be warned, though. Despite all the science, immediately after you decide your specifications you are all too likely to fall in love with a barge with all the wrong measurements. Only you can deal with that problem.

TYPES OF BARGE

We will talk in detail about only British and Dutch barges. This is not because we are biased – it is just that these are the only nationalities of barge you are likely to come across in the size you want.

We will also limit ourselves to metal (iron or steel) craft. Wooden barges are rare now because they are difficult and expensive to maintain.

BRITISH

Almost no barges for commercial inland work have been built in Britain since the1950s, and very few are still in trade now.

English barge waterways comprise a collection of canal and river navigations mostly grouped around the Thames, Severn, Mersey or Humber. Each group evolved its own varieties of craft. The principal types you might still find are the Leeds and Liverpool Canal short boats (but not many are left) and the Yorkshire keels. A good many ex-sailing or motor keels still exist.

English barges have a reputation for toughness. Keels, for example, were designed to trade on the north-eastern waterways, many of which are tidal, and typical standard form was (and still is) to race down the Trent on the ebb until there was too little water left to float in. The vessel would then rest on its chosen shoal with the crew slumbering until the grating of gravel on the bottom signalled refloating on the flood and time to get up and get moving again. Obviously, the vessels needed to be strong to survive this type of regular treatment.

Keels were built to a very bluff and quite deep design for maximum capacity, and to a number of standard sets of dimensions. Contrastingly, the short boats are basin-shaped craft, with shallow hulls. A craft of similar size, but slightly different character, developed on the (southern) Irish canals, and a few of these can still be found, but rarely unconverted. Other types of British barge which occasionally crop up include coasting ones (such as the famous Thames sailing barges, which fit in almost none of the UK canals), the vanishing rare Norfolk wherries, and various varieties of Mersey, Weaver and Manchester Ship Canal barges.

Most English barges were run by shore-based crews as opposed to families living on board, and were owned by carrying firms. These craft were working implements only, and as such were usually not subject to much of the loving care bestowed on the family-run long distance narrowboats or most Dutch vessels. For this reason, many English barges, while very rugged, tend to show neglect evidenced by pitted metalwork, numerous dents, and significant internal hull and frame corrosion.

In many ways these battle scars form part of the character of the vessel and add to its appeal, but equally they can make conversion and maintenance difficult indeed.

DUTCH

The Netherlands has been riddled with barges for several centuries. Every area developed its own types and hybrids.

However, since the 1950s, the Dutch government intervened in an attempt to make the barge trade more economic. It offered to buy, at attractive prices, small barges still carrying. It scrapped many it bought. It also offered compensation to barge owners to take them out of freight-carrying and convert them into something else – one reason for the many barge houseboats in the Netherlands. This means there are very few unconverted small Dutch barges still around.

Dutch barges were in general much more lightly built than English ones. It was not normal for ships to take the bottom fully loaded. The waterways were more often of uniform uncluttered depth, and capacity took precedence over strength. Whereas standard plating thickness for a 50T Yorkshire keel would be 10mm, a 250T Dutch luxe motor would be built in a mixture of 6mm and 8mm plating. The Dutch vessel's frames would be closer together but much smaller than in the English counterpart.

For this reason, allowing a Dutch barge to take the bottom regularly on a drying mooring requires caution. Soft mud does little harm, but hard uneven river bottoms do stress a hull, particularly where wash or wave conditions cause jarring as the vessel settles and rises on each tide. Thames sailing barges could dry out with a high degree of impunity, sometimes taking up alarming shapes but springing back to normal as soon as they floated. A Dutch barge will flex too, but not necessarily fully resume its previous shape afterwards.

On the other hand, many Dutch craft have been family-owned and run, and the subject of fanatical pride. This shows in their condition. Deterioration through internal corrosion is rare on a boat which recently traded, or at least it will be confined to isolated and usually predictable areas such as the aft end of the hold. Any dents sustained were normally ironed out rapidly before other skippers noticed them. Of course, examples of poor maintenance exist, and some Dutch barges used for day-boat gravel haulage etc. suffered as a result as they were unloaded by grab and often had wet holds. It is worth checking a craft's history if possible.

Some examples of hull shapes, British and Dutch.

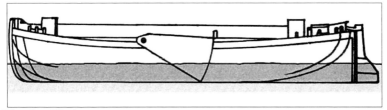

Humber Keel

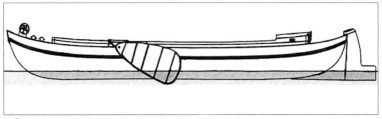

Aak

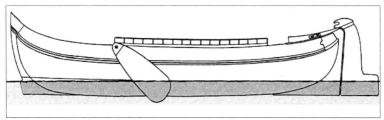

Tjalk

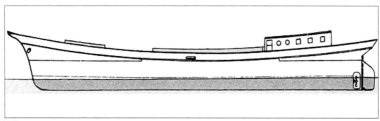

Klipper

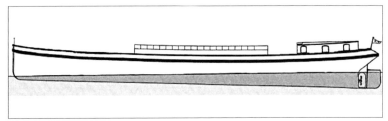

Katwijker

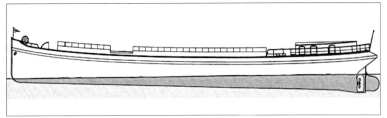

Motor barge, such as Steilsteven, Beurtschip, Luxe motor

All Dutch barges have individual characters which can never be recreated in a new vessel. Nevertheless, there is a strong trend now towards new build motor barges, both in England and the Netherlands. The Dutch have been building replica sailing vessels for years, but turned to motor ones only recently. A replica offers the reassurance of a modern welded hull, with massive frames and thick plating, so it can take the bottom and bounce through bridge holes with impunity. Below the water line, the hull form may be more simply shaped than a riveted original, as this is a cheaper way to build, although there are yards which will build exact copies for eye-watering prices.

So much for the principal differences between British and Dutch craft. Now to enter the minefield of the classes of Dutch barge.

The Dutch do not have a generic name for inland craft which equates to 'barge'. The nearest is 'binnenvaartschip' – inland transport ship (as opposed to 'grotevaartschip' or deep water ship). Although English has more terms for barge types than most people might think (wherry, short boat, hopper, Tom Pudding, pan, lighter, keel etc.) the Dutch have far more than the Brits do. Dutch craft are usually named according to one or more of four parameters: shape or style, size, area of origin, or function. We will start with some general descriptions of common styles.

AAK

Take a fairly parallel-sided marrow, cut it in half lengthwise, keep one half, and scoop out all the flesh. Put it on the table and squash it down a bit so the bottom is fairly flat and each end is slightly higher than the sides. Now you've got the basic shape of an aak (and a messy inedible marrow).

At the back, put a small triangle standing vertically, forming a slightly raked sternpost to hang the rudder on. Give it fore, aft and side decks set down a little from the rim of the shell, and hatch coamings standing up to form the hold opening. Set a mast at the front of the hatches, and lee boards each side. Perhaps add a bowsprit, and then give it cutter rig with the main-sail on a gaff and boom.

Some aak variants are hasselteraak, ijsselaak, zandaak, and rijtaak,. Nor should we forget the Dorstense aak, the keen or the herna. However, you probably should not worry too much about this for now – it is more like the difference between an MG TD and MG TF for car enthusiasts.

HAGENAAR

The hagenaar, basically an aak, is an example of a craft named for its area
of origin – Den Haag. The size of the hagenaar was determined by the 4.20m wide Wagenbrug ('brug' is bridge in Dutch) at Den Haag. This is a common beam for Dutch craft. Luckily for those wanting to cruise in Britain, it is just narrower than the somewhat standard 14 ft beam of many UK 'broad' locks.

TJALK (pronounced 'chal'k')

Take your aak and raise the deck to the top of the shell. Add a stem post and give it new bulwarks which lean inwards slightly, especially at the front and back. You have a thing that looks more or less like a clog – that is your basic tjalk. Your lifesize one will probably be more heavily built than the aak.

There are various types of tjalk. The paviljoentjalk, for example, has lovely stern cabins with sternward facing windows.

WESTLANDER

The westlander is named for its province of origin but can also be the generic description of low hulled barges . Originally built of wood, Westlanders were used to carry fruit and vegetables, but also sand, stone and manure. A Westlander looks something like a tjalk with its bow pushed slightly in. They are generally small barges, which loaded 10-40T.

Tjalk types often offer a good potential for a spacious conversion in the smaller sizes, since a larger cabin, if sympathetically built, can more easily be in keeping with the original style. However, the smaller sizes will also tend to have been out of trade for a longer time, implying a longer period in private ownership and perhaps possibly a longer period of neglect.

KLIPPER

Take a tjalk and press the sides of the fore-end so it is more pointed, then make the stempost and bulwarks flare out rather than lean in until the bow looks something like that on a sailing tea clipper. You have got the beginnings of a klipper.

Sailing klippers may come with one or two (or even three) masts. Again there are sub-types: Noordzee-klipper or Schoeneraak, Klipperaak, etc.

STEILSTEVEN

The word means 'straight stemmed', and these barges do indeed have vertical stem posts. The steilsteven stern is rounded and similar to that of an aak, but the curves are less extreme. As with the aak, there is usually no structural stern post, with, as for the aak bow, the keel plate simply carrying on up to the deck. An external sternpost is fitted to carry the rudder, and latterly the propeller.

Overall,Steilstevens have particularly subtle and elegant lines and are highly prized. They originated as sailing craft in Friesland and Groningen and were often engaged solely in the sugar beet and potato trade, being tied up for the rest of the year. They were easier and cheaper to build than a tjalk or aak, without loss of carrying capacity. They might be engaged solely in day trade, or fitted with a luxury stern cabin. Sometimes they had both motor and sails, and particularly heavily-built versions worked in the North and Baltic seas.

The types described above were almost all originally sailing craft. As such, they are often more satisfactory for work in more exposed waters; some types were specifically built for trading at sea. However, Dutch tidal estuaries and the Ijsselmeer are shallow, and conditions in such waters can deteriorate rapidly, imposing substantial demands upon any vessel. Be careful – the presence of a sailing rig on a barge does not indicate its capability to handle blue water.

LUXEMOTOR

Many non-Dutch enthusiasts fall in love with Luxemotors, which is fortunate because most Dutch prefer more traditional sailing craft. The Luxemotor was among the first of the purpose-built motor barges and may be considered an evolution of the Steilsteven. Most date from the 1920s. A Luxemotor usually has a proper engine room separated by full bulkheads, and superior stern living quarters which often were wonderfully fitted with varnished wood and etched glass.
They vary greatly in size, from 15m to 38m or more.

The Luxemotor hull usually has a sweeping counter stern (which reminds some people of the Titanic) and a straight-stemmed bow.

BEURT(MOTOR)SCHIP

Beurtschip means literally 'regular ship', a functional name describing vessels engaged in a regular scheduled service, particularly around Friesland, as opposed to the more common bulk cargo carriers. They were originally built as Tjalks, and eventually as a variant of Steilsteven and then Luxemotor. These were the workhorses of Friesland. They usually have a fairly small wheelhouse more or less right at the back. The accommodation was originally in the bow, with an entrance and skylight in the fore-deck, and sometimes a small porthole in the hull plating to give further light and ventilation. They mostly had a single hold, and a mast sprit-rigged on the fore-deck for self-discharging cargo.

The fore-end bulwark (the small fence usually found around the bow above deck level to stop you falling off the front, and sometimes along the sides and back as well) commonly continues with a toe rail where it joins the fore-deck; there is often a similar rail about 30cm high around the stern-end coming forward as far as the rear bollards next to the steering position.

They usually lacked the saloon roef (stern cabin), being used as day boats on regular scheduled runs. A flat stern deck took its place.

They were generally motor craft, and loaded from 50T to 250T. Many beurt-motorschips have finished up as bunker boats, little tankers serving ships and bulk cargo vessels – further definitions by function.

KATWIJKER

Another motor-barge type, this is named after the town of Katwijk which had a particularly low bridge with an air draft of 1.80m. This forced the katwijker to have a very shallow hold, a low demountable wheelhouse, a horizontal steering wheel (many have since been replaced by vertical ones), a gear lever with a removable top, and a bow the top of which could be unbolted and removed, all to reduce air draft. The other obvious distinguishing feature is a very wide rubbing band all round the gunwale, originally of timber clenched in metal though the timber has long since rotted away in most. This is ideally suited for hanging up the barge on the lock side as the water level drops!

A NOTE ON SEAWORTHINESS

Most Luxemotors and similar motor barges will hold their own at sea in calm weather conditions, usually with a stipulation of winds no stronger than force 4. However, even in force 3 or 4 winds, or less if there is a chop, motor barges can roll very uncomfortably if they take waves on the beam.

These barges can make coastal journeys, in suitable weather, only if properly prepared, your insurance company has been consulted and the skipper (or his pilot) has the necessary skill, knowledge and judgement. But they should not be thought of as sea-going craft. A lot of extra time must be allowed for any barge sea trip as you must wait for the right weather. You should never be driven to sea by impatience, supported by unsubstantiated hope that the wind will drop, or not rise, after you leave port.

SAIL OR MOTOR?

You can see from the types of barge described that many were originally built to sail, or were derived from sailing designs. Furthermore, there are now quite a few successful conversions to sail of Luxemotors, which as their name suggests were not originally intended for wind propulsion.

In fact, barges sail surprisingly well, being manoeuvrable, easy to handle (the Thames spritsail barge had a crew of one man and one boy), and steady. Because most have leeboards (drop keels on each side of the hull), sailing is not prejudiced by their shallow draft. They can be unexpectedly fast. Try a day on the Humber in Keels 'Comrade' or 'Amy Howson', particularly in a stiff breeze. These are restored keels (square rigged) and sloop (fore-and-aft rigged) respectively, both available for charter. You may be amazed how an apparently square chunk of iron can charge along with only the wind for power. Thames sailing barges are also available for charter such as https://www.top-sail.co.uk and in the Netherlands the 'brown fleet' comprise a huge number of charter barges - for example - https://www.egasail.com/brown-fleet-sailing .

Barges which sail are usually readily available on the market. They have many advantages (the challenge of sailing, the silent progress, the beauty of the rig). However, do not let that blind you to their disadvantages. They have all the capital and maintenance costs of a motor barge plus those of the rig. Although the masts of most are counterbalanced and can be lowered quickly, the rig can get in the way if you want to take them inland, and is often best removed from the barge and stored on the bank somewhere safe when you leave wider waters. And you usually have to demount any wheelhouse (which, in fact, many sailing barges do not have, as they would get in the way of the rig) when you are sailing, fully exposing you to the weather. We do not want to discourage you from buying a sailing barge, but do urge you to make a realistic estimate of how often you will actually sail, as opposed to motor, before you decide.

One last thought. Barges which originally sailed may not work under power as successfully as vessels designed to motor. Many Tjalks, for example, are of shallow draft with rounded hulls, and side slip considerably on corners and in windy conditions. You may find you need to use the lee boards for adequate control in some circumstances, if they have been retained. If they have been removed handling can be improved by adding bilge keels over 2/3rds on the length. The shape of these hulls can also make it difficult to install a bow thruster (see below).

EQUIPMENT

To a newcomer to the scene, a barge seems to contain a large and bewildering collection of unfamiliar and often greasy apparatus. This tends to generate an unpleasant feeling. You know that all this stuff is probably essential. But you barely know what it does, let alone whether the barge you are looking at has all the necessary bits, or whether anything vital is missing and may need to be purchased expensively later, whether the bits which are there carry respected brands, and whether they are in good enough condition.

There is no easy answer to this, and even those more familiar with barges can be confronted with types of equipment they have never come across before, made by manufacturers they have never heard of. Even a long-term owner might not be able to find their way around other engine rooms, particularly those representing several layers of marine engineering archaeology and the combined efforts of a number of previous 'practical boat owners'. In addition all owners have their own view about what is necessary and what can be dispensed with – views likely to be influenced by what is in the barge they are trying to sell to you.

Cheer up, though. We will take you through the basics, which should at least arm you with some of the right questions to ask as you peer into an engine room full of strange-looking machinery. It will not take as long as you might think to gain confidence.

Engine Room

Even if you want a totally immobile barge, you may still end up with the remains of an engine room, so this seems to be the place to start.

2-cylinder, air start Deutz, c1936

You will soon see that it is not only the engine that lives there. You will often find all sorts of other pieces of equipment to do with pushing the barge through the water, as well as machinery for generating electricity and heat, and other items from storage shelves to work benches.
Never think that once you ave seen one engine room you have seen them all. Barges were not usually built according to detailed plans in the first place, and have often been altered since birth, so engine rooms tend to be

as individual as their previous owners, and may give you an interesting lesson on the vessel's history. Although the excellent design and immaculate condition of the accommodation may impress you, the engine room may reveal a totally different aspect to the ship.

A motor barge tends to have a purpose-built engine room. It is usually easy to enter and spacious, with standing headroom, due to the fact that the original engine of maybe 15kW probably took up four times the space as does the more modern 90kW machine now ensconced. Typically the original engine room was a space between two watertight bulkheads in front of the aft cabin, or between a bulkhead and the stern of the barge. In either case, this may have made it difficult to reduce its size when a smaller machine was fitted later, as moving a watertight bulkhead is not something you do in an afternoon.

In a sailing barge, space simply had to be found when an engine was added. In some cases the whole aft space under the deck was used. In others, the engine was put ahead of the original aft accommodation bulkhead and a second bulkhead fitted ahead of it to make a watertight engine room. In either case, the headroom may be restricted, and can even be as low as the engine itself, giving more of an engine space than a room.

Service work and repairs are obviously more easily done in a spacious engine room where you do not have to crawl through small holes, develop a hunch back, or lie in the bilge to do the job. However, other considerations creep in.

Your equipment may require less frequent maintenance than that built in the early 1900s, and you probably want to use as much as possible of the space on board for your accommodation. A big engine room may seem a bit wasteful in this light. It is possible to provide reasonable access to all the necessary machinery in quite a small space if it is well laid out, but sadly this has not always been achieved in non-original engine rooms.

When you are cruising, the engine room is the place where the noise and fumes are created. It is a good idea if you can keep them there: a fully isolated space is an advantage. This enhances fire safety too. Also, the ship's engineers need to get in and out of the engine room at times under way, when it is dark, the ship is rolling and the engine is running. Access should be convenient and wide enough, and your part of the engine room well lit and clear of hot exhaust pipes and bits of moving machinery.

A final point to consider when looking at the engine room architecture is what happens if you have to get the engine out of its home. How easy is it (or is it possible at all) to lift it straight out with a crane? Can you get it out with all its accessories fitted or will you first need to dismantle it partially in place and take the gearbox off (no fun at all)? In some cases ambitious owners get carried away with their conversions, and when the engine needs an overhaul they first have to cut away chunks of pretty steel work and demolish whole galleys, bathrooms, or whatever.

The engine

In most cases, you will want a barge that moves under its own power, so let us deal with the engine itself.

Barge engines are almost invariably diesels. Diesel engines are well suited to this purpose because of their greater durability compared to petrol (gasoline) engines, their fuel economy, and their limited need for electrical accessories.

You may be surprised at how small barge engines are. Even a 30m vessel may have only a 90kW unit (one horsepower is 0.75kW). A 20m vessel may happily get by with half that. This is because it takes unexpectedly little energy to move a barge through the water, particularly at walking pace – which is the normal top speed. In fact, even engines of these sizes are usually just loafing along during the average cruise as they now may have to shift as little as 10T of conversion, furniture and passengers as opposed to the 100T of cargo which they used to carry.

For a barge with a typical conversion used for cruising on average inland waters (not, for example, in the strong current of the Rhine at Koblenz), the minimum engine size required can be roughly estimated using the following rule of thumb:

length (m) x beam (m) x 0.75 = power required (kW).

The main reason for having even this much power is in case you need to stop or turn in a hurry, although it does not always help as much as you hope. Some of the old barge masters may have got along with only 30kW in the engine room, but they tended to know more handling tricks than do most of today's leisure skippers. An added safety margin of power makes good sense.

You might think that a more powerful engine would be much thirstier than a small one, but in fact the amount of fuel used relates more closely to the amount of work done than to engine size. Most (unladen small) barges burn something like four to five litres of diesel fuel an hour at normal speeds (under 10km/hour), no matter what engine they have. Almost every type and make of diesel engine has been put into some barge somewhere, so you will come across a varied selection. They can be broken down into the following categories.

Vintage engine

The first engines were put into barges over 90 years ago, and some of them are still running just fine. These were typically physically large (e.g.7-litre) machines, very slow running (perhaps 600 revs/minute maximum), and not very powerful (some as little as 15kW) but with a lot of torque. They were simple and built to last. And they do. Such an engine often has one huge vertical cylinder. They are almost always water-cooled. Manufacturers of such engines which you may come across include Kromhout, Deutz, Industrie, and Klöckner. (UK canal boat enthusiasts may realise we are talking about something similar to a large equivalent of the Bolinders found in narrowboats.) However, these engines lack refinements we take for granted with modern machines. For example, early engines were often semi-diesels, which means they can run only if they are hot. To start one from cold means playing a blowlamp over the top of the engine for 10 minutes or so then turning it over (often by hand or by foot). As a result, once going, they are kept running all the time unless the vessel is going to be tied up for a couple of hours or more.

It is quite feasible still to run a barge with such an engine. It adds a special character to the vessel, and its engine room can be the owner's pride and joy. However, as we have already suggested, these are large machines and take up a lot of valuable space, and will be under-powered for some waters; they are less convenient than modern engines and require more attention to run. Although more spare parts may be available than you might expect, you may have to have some specially made to fix a break-down. On the other hand they are reliable and seem likely to last forever, and nothing can match the sound of their slow exhaust beat.

Some of these engines have no electrical accessories at all, especially, no electric starter. There may be a mechanical starting system powered by compressed air, though. An airpump recharges the air bottle once the engine is running. This type of system is fine but its plumbing may look a little daunting.

We do not want to put you off a vintage engine, just to make you aware of what having one might entail. The modern bargee and the classic boat enthusiast in you might run into a conflict of interest should you find one of those artefacts of industrial history in the boat of your desire. You just want to be able to turn the key and leave the wharf, but would you rip out an original Boxer engine from a 1960 Porsche to replace it with a Suzuki 3-cylinder just to have a unit for which you can get spare parts easily? If yes, before you scrap the old lady, get in touch with somebody who might give her a new home. Museums and enthusiast clubs are often happy to take them in, or to help find someone who will.

Classic engine

The next age of barge engines brought the first true diesels (no blowlamps here). They, too, are big heavy machines but usually with two or four cylinders. They are also slow running, but not nearly as slow as the semi-diesels. They started appearing in the 1920s, and their era virtually drew to an end in the 1950s (although some are still made). They are more powerful than vintage engines – but not necessarily a lot more. They, too, are usually water-cooled.

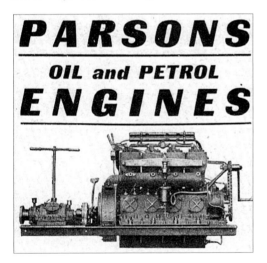

They are somewhat more sophisticated than the vintage engines, but may also have primitive features. For example, most have electric start but others must still be started manually. The spare parts situation is similar to that of the vintage engines: you may need to become a member of the enthusiasts' organisation for the brand of engine concerned.

These engines are gaining the same degree of cachet that the hot-bulbs have had for some time. They are machines with a following, and can add to the atmosphere of your craft. But the same provisos apply to them as suggested earlier for vintage engines.

Modern engine

'Modern' engines may be 30 or more years old (if such an engine is well maintained, it should be able to withstand the relatively light demands of powering a barge for a very long time).

These are still 'industrial' engines, but more sophisticated than the classics. They will usually be four or six cylinder units, with maximum turning speeds of 1,800 to 2,600 rev/minute.

Most are water-cooled, but you may come across an air-cooled one. There are many acceptable brands, from those more familiar to people in the UK (such as Cummins, Ford, Lister, Perkins, and Mercedes-Benz) to others more common in mainland Europe (Deutz, Hanomag, and Scania).

Some think the very best were made by Gardner, a UK company. Gardners have a reputation for very high quality, durability and fuel economy. Some were made under licence in the Netherlands by Kromhout. But beware! Parts may not be interchangeable between English and Dutch versions.

In the last 25 years or so, it has become common to use engines taken out of road vehicles. In the Netherlands, the overwhelming favourite was the DAF 6-cylinder, with power ratings from 65kW to 80kW. There is nothing essentially wrong with this approach, provided the engine has been properly marinised and installed. However, the engine may have been (much) used on the road before it came aboard, so a careful assessment of remaining life is in order. Common engines like the DAF may be bigger than really needed. A major advantage of this style of engine is that parts can often be found in road vehicle wrecking yards.

New (to you)

The barge you love may have a completely hopeless engine, or even none at all. This need not necessarily rule out a purchase. Install your own.

The easiest way to get an engine is to go to any manufacturer or supplier of marine engines, buy everything you need off the shelf and get the supplier to install it. Easy, but you may be looking at £12,000 to £15,000 for a 6-cylinder unit. On the other hand, you could get a truck engine, have it reconditioned and marinised by a specialist marine engineer who will probably be more than happy to install it for you as well. This could set you back between £5,000 and £10,000 depending on work and parts required. Finally, you could buy a used marine engine and overhaul it for between £3,000 and £7,000.(Feb 2022 prices)

However if your ship needs a European Certificate (required if 20m or more length overall or Length x Beam X Maximum Draft in metres is 100 or over) to cruise in mainland Europe then you can only re-engine with specific low emission engines. Emission limits for inland waterway vessels were significantly tightened under the Stage V regulation. The Stage V limits are applicable to propulsion (IWP) and auxiliary (IWA) engines above 19 kW. There is, however, a considerable after-market in 'short' engines enabling you to refurbish your existing elderly DAF or similar.

ENGINE INSTALLATION

An engine for a barge must first be made suitable for use afloat, a process called 'marinisation', then properly installed in the vessel.

Marinisation involves adding the necessary bits to an engine to enable it to work in a ship. There can be more to this than you expect. The essential elements are a cooling system and a connection between the engine and the drive (gearbox, propeller shaft, etc.), but there are other things which (some) engines need – such as instruments, special exhausts, fuel systems, starters, alternators and heavier flywheels. Some engines even need new oil pumps and sumps because they are mounted at different angles in boats from trucks.

A marine engine should, by definition, arrive already professionally marinised. An engine originally in a road vehicle, however, will have had the marine equipment added later, with potential for things to have gone awry. As often in life, there is an important difference between a proper job and botching. You can often spot the latter quite easily by looking at the general state of fabrication and the quality of the components. Some have even retained the former truck cooling fan and radiator! But others are more difficult to detect, where the key bits are the ones you cannot see. Some DIY marinisations are done well, but beware those cobbled together on the cheap.

COOLING

There are two basic ways of cooling the engine: air and water.

A few Hanomags, Listers and Deutzs are still around which use large fans to blow air round the engine (although nearly all propulsion engines in barges are water-cooled these days). An air-cooled engine does not need as much pipe work, it avoids the risk of freezing up in winter and – most usefully – does not have raw water inlet filters (which are liable to get clogged and allow overheating). On the other hand, these engines tend to be noisy. Also, they need to draw cool air from the outside, requiring air ducts and shrouds round the engine. These tend to clutter up the space and can make access difficult for engine maintenance. Water-cooling comes in several variants. The most primitive uses direct raw water: water in which the barge is floating is drawn in through a hull fitting, pumped through the engine and then dumped overboard. Although this system does work, the water may not be the cleanest (and certainly will not contain anti-freeze) so is not really recommended.

A better approach is indirect cooling, where the raw water passes through a heat exchanger which fulfils the same role as the radiator in a car. The engine coolant (which should have anti-freeze in it) is inside the heat exchanger, and goes round the engine in a separate sealed circuit.

Another variant is skin tank cooling, in which no external water is drawn inboard. The heat exchanger is a large flat tank welded on to the inside of an underwater section of the hull: heat escapes through the hull. With this system it is vital to have a sufficiently large cooling surface area, and proper baffles in the hull tank. However, if the tank is too small, a second can normally be added without too much difficulty if there is enough spare and accessible hull surface inside. Unfortunately though, it is quite difficult to install a skin tank successfully in a riveted hull due to the hull's irregular surface.

Finally, there is keel cooling. The skin tank is replaced by a heat exchanger comprising pipes immersed in cool water outside the hull. But these can be vulnerable and may pose a problem in shallow waters or on a drying mooring. More sophisticated is an open-sided steel box, smaller than a skin tank and let into the hull, inside which is a finned heat exchanger immersed in raw water – Blokland is one of the well-known makes.

It is usually possible, and need not be too expensive, to change the water cooling method (but not to change from air to water!). You can convert from direct to indirect, but if you plan to do so remember to budget for it in the purchase cost.

EXHAUST

Yet again you will find alternative ways of dealing with a requirement, in this case getting your exhaust fumes outboard.

The principal choice is between wet and dry. (No, this is not like the sandpaper that works both ways.) Either approach is acceptable.

A dry exhaust is like those used in cars. The exhaust gas goes out of the engine (manifold) into a pipe, through a muffler (silencer), and out through a hole in the hull or through the deck into a vertical exhaust pipe.

The wet exhaust uses the raw engine cooling water after it has cooled the engine. This is injected into the exhaust pipe to cool the gases. It uses a different type of muffler, often rubber.

Dry exhausts are simpler, but are much hotter and so require insulation (lagging) to prevent injury to the crew and too much heat in the engine room. They also tend to be noisier than wet ones. On the other hand, a wet exhaust requires a water supply. It requires more maintenance (it may need draining for winter lay-up to avoid freezing). It must be installed so that water cannot siphon back from outside the hull and flood the engine – or even sink the vessel. And if the water supply fails (clogs), that nice rubber muffler may melt. An overheat alarm is useful.

ENGINE INSTRUMENTS

Engines need instruments so the steerer can keep in touch with what is going on, out of sight, in the engine room. In some barges originally built for sail, the instruments are very inconveniently located and you may not even be able to see them when at the helm. Not a good thing. Other instrument panels may be very sparse. At minimum you need a tachometer, running hours meter, temperature gauge and oil pressure gauge. High temperature and low oil pressure warning lights and alarms are very worthwhile. A fuel gauge is handy (but often absent) and EU certificated boats are required to have an audible low fuel alarm. There should at least be a volt meter for each DC electrical system. The instruments should have lights for night operation. The engine stop control should be very convenient to operate in case of emergencies.

MOUNTING

There are two main choices in installing an engine in a barge: solid or flexible mounting.

With solid mounting, the engine feet (part of the marinisation) are bolted straight on to the engine bed (heavy steel members usually welded to the hull). The advantage of this is that once everything is lined up and bolted down, it is nearly trouble-free. The disadvantage is that the engine vibrations and noises travel down the mounting into the hull. Most vintage and classic engines have to be on solid mountings.

Flexible mounting is used to reduce the noise. The engine feet sit on (relatively) soft blocks, which themselves are bolted to the engine bed. This does reduce vibration transmission, but unavoidably allows the engine to move about somewhat. To allow for the movement, there must be some kind of joint (there are several types) in the propeller shaft, usually incorporating a thrust bearing, and a flexible bellows in the exhaust system. This is a more complicated approach but the noise reduction can be worthwhile.

Unfortunately, we are talking dynamics here, a complex field, and you may still get strange noises and even damaging vibrations at certain speeds. These can require an expert to remedy.

A final consideration relates to the environment. You rarely find a dry engine. They always seem to drip oil or diesel. Even if yours is completely dry, it is almost guaranteed that you will spill some oil during a change or some diesel when bleeding the system. This will dribble down and collect at the lowest point. If this is the same point where bilge water collects (such as the small amount which always drips through even a healthy stern gland, for example), there is a problem as the resulting mixture must not be pumped overboard. Ideally, there should be a drip tray under the engine. However, many older installations do not include one, and it can be very awkward to put one in after the fact. In that situation, the bilge under the engine should be separated from the rest of the bilge by a bulkhead or dam. Today's regulations require one or other of these approaches, but an older installation may still not have one and so not
pass an official inspection.

FUEL SUPPLY

Engines need fuel, and there are important considerations here. First, what type of fuel? Diesel is used almost universally. But there are two types: red (which is dyed) and white (colourless). White is about twice as expensive in UK as red because its price includes road tax – other countries have a smaller differential. This is what trucks and diesel cars use.

Barges are allowed to use red diesel for propulsion engines in UK but have to pay for the propulsion fuel at the full duty rate. In the EU (and including Northern Ireland) barges must now use white diesel for main engines and are only allowed to use red diesel for generating electricity, for heating and cooking (HLP). Hydrotreated Vegetable Oil (HVO) is the most recent diesel alternative and very attractive due to its low emissions and long storage life – however it has a price premium of at least 10% over conventional diesel. Red HVO can be used for HLP and white, full duty paid, for propulsion in many – but not all countries – see www.barges.org for news as this fuel becomes more widely available.

This means that your barge, ideally, should have two fuel tanks, one for red and one for white. If it does not, do not rule it out. Adding an extra tank is not that difficult provided there is room.

Tanks are usually made of steel and left untreated on the inside. Yes, they do rust inside in time, especially if they are not kept well filled. Stainless steel tanks, or even (special) fabric ones, will not rust but are fairly rare.

How big should the tanks be? The larger they are, the less often you have to refuel. Apart from being more convenient, large tanks allow you to travel with less worry in areas (such as many parts of rural France, for example) where fuelling points are widely separated. However, there is a trade off between space for tanks and that for accommodation. A 500 litre tank will allow you to cruise for about 100 hours between refuellings.

Diesel fuel floats on water, so condensation inside the tank collects at the bottom. This should be removed once in a while, which requires a drain cock right at the bottom of the tank. There should also be cocks in the fuel lines to allow the fuel to be shut off for repairs or in an emergency. A remote shut-off outside the engine room, ideally accessible from the helm, is a good safety feature but often absent. Each tank needs a breather (an air pipe out of the top of the tank) which must vent outside the hull and should be above the level of the filler cap. A level indicator is handy, but glass or plastic sight glasses (vertical tubes at tank level) are now outlawed in most countries; gauges or dip sticks are usual.

It is essential for the fuel to be filtered on its way from tank to engine. If the filtration is not good enough, you soon have expensive problems with the injectors or other equipment. Two types of filter are needed. First, a sedimenter or water trap – basically a sealed bowl with an inlet and outlet at the top. The bowl is removed occasionally to empty out any nasty stuff which has collected in it. Second, one or more fine filters. These are usually attached to the engine itself and take the form of replaceable cartridges. All filters should be easy to get at. Best practice is two fuel supply pipes, each with filters, so if one gets clogged (and stops the engine, always at the most inconvenient time!) you can immediately switch to the other while you replace the clogged filters. A common cause of clogging is rust washing off the inside of the fuel tanks during a passage through rough water.

Another type of fuel tank you may find is a day tank – a small tank mounted high up, and usually holding about a day's consumption of fuel. Typically it is connected to the main tank via a hand pump. Historically it was used as a further measure for filtering the diesel. Also, older engine types often required a gravity fuel feed, which meant a tank above the engine. Today we can do without day tanks since diesel is cleaner, filters are more effective and automatic fuel lifting pumps are almost universal. But they do no harm.

Diesel fuel is inherently safe as it is quite hard to get it to burn or explode, but regulations are tightening up. We won't attempt to tell you all the current rules but it is usually quite easy to comply with them by making relatively minor changes to the installed fuel system and you will find more information on the regulations at www.barges.org.

DRIVE

For the engine to move the barge, its power has to be converted into a push against the water. There are a number of elements making up the 'drive': the gearbox or transmission, the shaft, and the propeller.

The functions of the transmission are to deliver the engine power to the shaft; to make the shaft rotate in forward, reverse, or not at all (neutral); and to make the shaft spin more slowly than the engine ('reduction'). Large slow-turning propellers are more efficient than smaller ones turning at engine speed.

The conventional approach is a marine gearbox bolted to a bell-shaped housing at the flywheel end of the engine. The gearbox power input shaft engages with a drive plate (where a clutch would be in a car). At the other end of the gearbox its output shaft is connected to the inboard end of the propeller shaft.

Marine gearboxes have to be very tough. They take all the shocks of going into forward and reverse (changes often made far too quickly), and those of the propeller hitting something solid. Often they incorporate the thrust bearing, which is the bit of the barge the propeller shaft pushes against to make the barge move (but if not there should be a stand-alone thrust bearing somewhere along the propeller shaft). However, there comes a time when even the best gearbox cannot stand any more (ab)use, so any strange gearbox noises should definitely worry you. They are expensive (£1,000 plus) to repair or replace, although there

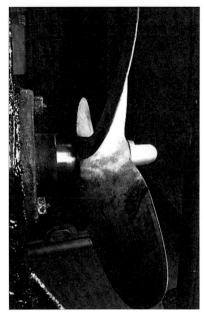

are specialist reconditioners who sometimes offer good deals on exchange units.

A gearbox is not the only option. Power can be transmitted successfully by hydraulics, electricity, or even in some rare cases belts.

Hydraulic drive is common in hire boats where the engine simply drives a hydraulic pump and the output can be used to drive a hydraulic motor directly attached to the propellor shaft. The advantage is that the engine can be placed athwartships and accessible through a deck hatch for easy replacement or repair and takes up less space. The hydraulic pump can also be used to drive a bow-thruster and anchor winches.

Electric drive is becoming a more popular option typically with a generator and solar for battery charging driving an electric motor. As with hydraulic on top of the green advantages the generator does not need to be adjacent to the motor. There are a number of companies now offering complete systems which could be a better option than a new low emission engine for retro-fitting.

Whatever the prime mover, the propeller shaft will be supported on one or more bearings. The stern tube bearing, typically a large brass bushing, will wear in time, particularly if it has been used in dirty water. Checking for this should be part of the survey. Just inboard of the stern tube bearing there will be a device (a grease-filled gland, for example) to preventing water from coming in.

Although the propeller is outside the engine room, it seems most sensible to deal with this item here. It is usually three- (occasionally four-) bladed, made of bronze or steel. Do not worry about which. It may be over 65 cm in diameter and be worth hundreds of pounds. Best if it is not too bent or chewed! Propeller sizes are specified in diameter x pitch (pitch is how far the propeller would theoretically screw forward through water in one revolution), and a replacement must have a hub big enough to accept the size of propeller shaft already installed. The propeller must be matched properly to both engine and drive if the engine is to work efficiently. This matching is rather a black art, but if the barge seems to go much too fast at the lowest engine speed or too slowly at the highest, or if it does not reach a normal engine speed when cruising, there is probably a mismatch. Seek specialist advice if you suspect this to be the case.

Some propeller suppliers have computer programs which calculate the specifications of propeller needed. In most cases they feed your data in free of charge in the hope of selling you a propeller. To save you a second call if you use this service, here is a list of information you will need to supply:
- Maximum engine revolutions/minute
- Engine power
- Drive reduction ratio
- Maximum diameter of the propeller you can accommodate
- Length and maximum beam at the waterline
- Draft (or, occasionally, displacement and maximum hull speed).

However, even with the services of a computer, the match may turn out to be not quite right, so adjust your expectations accordingly.

If there is a mismatch, correction may require installing a different propeller of the right size, the hub of which will probably need machining so that its mounting hole fits the shaft perfectly. Some propeller specialists can alter the diameter or pitch (or both!) of your propeller, which can be less expensive than getting a new one.

It is a feature of many barges that the stern moves sideways as well as backwards when the transmission is in reverse. This is called the 'paddle wheel effect', as it is caused by the propeller acting as a paddle wheel because the water pressure is lower at its top than its bottom. If the propeller is too near the surface of the water it can draw in air instead of water, losing effectiveness and possibly vibrating badly. Both these effects can be reduced by 'anti-ventilation' / 'anti-cavitation' plates, metal strips or a tube near the propeller. Unfortunately, these can make it difficult for you to fish with a boat hook to clear the inevitable rubbish that propellers attract (nothing is all to the good).

Although it is quite easy to move the stern sideways with the engine, moving the bow can be another story, particularly when space is limited, there is a cross wind and there are crushable small craft nearby. One answer is the bow thruster, a small propeller mounted cross-wise in a tube near the bow. This may be driven hydraulically from the main engine, electrically, or directly by its own small diesel engine. However, there are drawbacks here too. Bow thrusters are usually used only in short bursts, which can mean their diesel engines never warm up and may wear unusually quickly. Their propellers can suck in rubbish, which can do a lot of damage in the confining tube. For some types, the engine and tube can take up a significant amount of space which could otherwise provide highly desirable storage area or part of a cabin. A bow thruster is a very useful tool but if the purchase price is boosted because of it, make sure it works properly. Many barges do not have one.

NAVIGATION

STEERING

To cruise where you want to, you need to be able to point the barge in the right direction. Barges usually have large rudders to allow you to achieve this, but there are a few variations in how the rudder is moved.

Originally, barges (especially sailing barges) were steered by a tiller, a large wooden bar, often beautifully carved, attached to the top of the rudder.

Many older barges still are steered this way. Tiller steering is very direct and quick and requires little maintenance but is not universally loved. It can require considerable strength, especially in rough weather. And the steerer almost always has to stand outside, rain or shine.

Many barges originally steered by tillers have been converted to wheel steering. The rest had this from the start. The traditional approach is a large wheel which pulls the rudder by means of chains (or cables) connected to a quadrant on the rudder shaft. Nowadays, it is good safety practice (and the law in some countries) that the wheel have an outer rim attached to the end of the spokes if it is the of 'ship's wheel' type. You really do not want to have your arm (or anything else) between the spokes if the rudder hits something hard or meets a large wave.

Chain steering is perfectly all right but can be a little heavy if it takes only a few turns of the wheel to go from full starboard to full port. You do not want there to be too many turns, as this can slow you down seriously in emergency manoeuvring.

Another option is hydraulic steering, where a small hydraulic pump is attached to the wheel shaft and a ram to the rudder quadrant. This may require less space (and sometimes less maintenance) than a chain system.

Some hydraulic steering is powered, thus reducing the size of steerer's biceps required.
However, some powered hydraulic steering systems provide almost no feedback (feel as to what the rudder is doing), which can be disconcerting. Also, there is slightly more machinery which could break down. On the other hand, you can dispense with the wheel, replacing it with a joystick if you wish. A powered system does allow fairly easy fitting of an auto-pilot – invaluable if you are intending regular channel crossings or coastal passages.

NAVIGATION INSTRUMENTS

Some barges have no navigation instruments because they have never needed them on the quiet inland routes. But you may be going farther afield, so if your purchase comes with a fuller inventory it could save you money later.

If you ever expect to be travelling in the dark, fog or snow, you will need navigation lights. Lights of the proper size for a barge cost more than you might think (plus installation, of course), so it is a definite plus if a barge already has them. The full set is port (red), starboard (green), stern (white pointing backwards), bow (white pointing forward), and anchor (white all around). A spotlight, and a headlight (for tunnels), are also recommended.

All barges must have an effective horn. These vary from the portable and mouth-operated to large air trumpets with their own compressors.

It is difficult nowadays to get away without a VHF radio. Many ports insist that vessels communicate with them by VHF, and you can save a lot of time by calling ahead when approaching one of the many locks which are VHF-equipped. In mainland Europe each VHF radio must automatically identify itself (ATIS and RAINWAT) at the start of each call; many older models cannot do this.

If you venture on to larger waters, you may need a compass. This is by no means a universal fitting. Additional navigation equipment could include global positioning equipment (GPS), chart-plotter, radar and depth sounder.

Automatic identification systems (AIS) transponders are designed to be capable of providing position, identification and other information about the ship to other ships and to coastal, harbour and lock authorities automatically. If your barge is over 20m and used in the EU it is compulsory to fit an AIS Inland or A transponder. Under this length it is optional but very useful and you can have the cheaper AIS B transponder. The transponder transmits your position, course, speed and vessel details on a dedicated VHF channel. The information can be displayed on a laptop with a suitable cable connection along with a chart display such as PC Navigo or OpenPCN.

Finally, have you wondered why our Association called its journal Blue Flag? A blue flag is a piece of equipment, peculiar to barges, which is essential if you use mainland Europe river navigations. A vessel coming upstream which wishes to pass 'on the wrong side' (i.e. starboard to starboard) to avoid heavy current can display a blue flag to indicate its intentions. Today this is no longer a flag but a scintillating white light on a tilting blue board usually mounted just outside the wheel house. For ships 20m and over the light is compulsory (CEVNI regulations) but the board is optional.

OTHER

An anchor is essential on rivers and tidal waters. You will need it if the engine fails for any reason. As you will not always be able to stop alongside a canal bank sometimes you will have to anchor. Each barge should have a suitable anchor (at the bow), a significant length of heavy chain, and a winch to get the whole lot back on board. A powered winch is a bonus (if it works properly) but a manual one can do the job just fine, if slowly. Another (usually smaller) anchor at the stern can be very handy too, especially for stopping in a hurry when heading downstream.

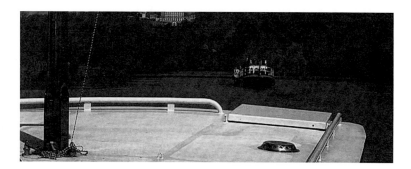

Towing a dinghy can cause problems, particularly in locks, so you need to be able to get the dinghy on board (and have somewhere to stow it). Traditional Dutch dinghies are made of steel and weigh just as much as you imagine. Even wooden dinghies can be hard to lift. A davit, a small crane for lifting dinghies, is a useful fitting. Modern inflatable dinghies are often light enough to launch and recover by hand.

And finally, the barge will need a suite of ropes of various sizes, for mooring, hanging on to bollards in locks, towing, etc. For mooring out in the country, you will need some long metal spikes to pound into the bank with a sledge hammer as temporary bollards.

SAFETY

Safety on the water is critical. You need to keep it in mind the entire time. Do not ever forget that a barge is a ship, not a floating apartment. A full discussion of safety does not belong in this handbook, but the following items are worth checking when you view barges.

You may need to escape from the vessel in a hurry if it starts to sink or catches fire. Does every room on board have adequate exits?

If the vessel gets into rough weather, waves may come over the top of the hull. Will the barge shed this water quickly and completely? If there is a well deck or cockpit, is it adequately drained?

Most barges were designed with water-tight bulkheads creating three or more separate compartments (bow, hold and stern). This would ensure that the barge remained afloat even if one compartment filled with water through swamping, collision or a leak. Conversion may have resulted in the piercing or removal of one or both bulkheads as they can limit interior layout flexibility and efficiency. This is not necessarily a problem, but you (and some insurers) may feel more comfortable if the bulkheads are still intact.

Any pipe can spring a leak, so every fitting which passes water through the hull under water must have a sea cock (shut off valve) immediately inside the hull. Check these and the condition of the hull fitting, as safety inspectors certainly will, and check that they work and are in good condition. Older or amateur conversions may have omitted them, they may be corroded, be in poor condition or set too close to the waterline. Failure of hull fittings and seacocks are one of the most common causes of serious water ingress, insurance claims and sinking!

In case water does start getting in, there must be ways of getting it out again. Bilge pumps vary in sophistication, from hand-operated to fully automatic electric. There should be at least one available in every watertight compartment, with a mix of electrical and mechanical (manual or directly driven by the engine) in case of electricity failure. Electric pumps with water-sensing switches are worth-while, particularly if you leave the barge unattended for longer periods. You do not want to come back and find it has sunk as the result of a small leak!

Finally, there is all the portable equipment, from one or more life rings to life jackets and emergency flares. A full list of the equipment required should be available from the local navigation authority and in the website Knowledge Base.

THE CONVERSION

Conversion makes a former freight-carrying barge suitable for cruising and living in. You may decide to convert your barge yourself (using your own hands or with the help of a boat builder or yard). However, very few barges are now available straight out of trade so you may have to remove an existing conversion and start again. This is quite feasible, and might be the only way to get the layout you want. It also allows you to stipulate the materials and quality of workmanship and to install new equipment. However, a substantial re-conversion may be much more expensive than retaining the existing conversion and making only minor alterations, so beware.

We should issue a general warning here. Work on barges always takes much longer and costs much more than you initially estimate – and more than equivalent work on land-based homes or equipment.

After those gloomy thoughts, we move on to the more uplifting questions of what you might want and look for in a conversion.

We assume you have now made the decisions as to what you want from the ship and where your main cruising ground will be. This is your basis for judging the conversion. Before you settle on what you actually need, answer questions such as:

• How many berths do you really need? (Cruising with large numbers on board can become somewhat tiring after a while)
• Must berths be in private bedrooms with an en-suite or can shared facilities be more appropriate

• Will you use the ship primarily for cruising, or mainly as a static residence with occasional trips?
   • Who will use the ship? How robust and able are they?
   • Will you be on board in winter?
   • What type of interior do you prefer (traditional, modern, light, dark, types of furnishing and fabrics)?
* What household equipment do you consider essential, and what would you prefer in an ideal world?

Try to look at as many interiors as possible. No two barges or conversions are the same. The more you see, the more interesting ideas you will come across. Most barge owners are only too happy to talk about and show off their vessels, and boat shows often have larger craft on display.

Do not forget that although hull, engine, navigation equipment etc. are all vital to any boat owner, if the ship fails to provide somewhere warm, dry, and inviting, with the potential for a hot meal after a long day's cruising, you probably will not be happy with it.

What follows is a brief description of the main elements of a conversion. Conversion merits a book of its own, so we have limited ourselves to hitting the high points – suggesting the principal choices you may come across and giving basic ideas on good practice.

Many buyers have undertaken a conversion, or made minor or even significant alterations to an existing conversion, after purchase. However, if you are thinking of this, do seek some experienced advice before buying. It may turn out that the changes you are thinking of will be rather more difficult to implement than you suspect. Many boatyards will give you some initial comments on what you want to do, and, if they think you really are serious, a rough idea of the expected cost of the work.

STARTING FROM THE OUTSIDE

The overall shape of the conversion governs what you can put in it and whether the barge looks right. An attractively shaped hull can be ruined by a clumsy cabin top. There are a lot of the latter, and they can be expensive to reshape. However, it is a matter of taste whether the top of the conversion is flat or follows the sheer (curve) of the hull. Either can look good.

Size of the conversion can vary considerably for a given hull. Some use virtually the entire length of the craft, maximising floor space while leaving just enough room outside to navigate the vessel (there really must be enough for safe working); others have spacious open decks for socialising in warm climes. Some have full-standing height throughout, others may have (for example) lower fore-cabins. Most are built on the original coamings (the raised metal edges around the hold which the hatch covers sit on), but some have achieved more interior room by narrowing the side decks.

Some ships have a wheelhouse which, in effect, adds another room and makes for pleasantly sociable cruising (but you lose its use if it is demounted). Others have a basic box with just enough room inside for the steerer. In mainland Europe, many wheelhouses are fixed, which can be a problem with the lower bridges found in the UK. Most wooden wheelhouses can be made demountable, but steel ones usually cannot – but there are innovative hydraulic powered retractable solutions.

Many conversions retain an original stern cabin behind a full-width engine room, with the bulk of the accommodation in the former hold, but this is by no means the only possibility. Although the original cabin can provide a completely separate room (or even a small suite), useful for privacy if you plan to run the barge on charter or want to get away from your guests when cruising, you may have to climb awkwardly through the wheelhouse to get to it. Not handy if the wheelhouse is demounted and it is raining.

Some types of barge allow for a passage past the engine room, linking bow and stern accommodation on one level. Others have the engine right at the stern, consolidating all the  accommodation forward. On most barges, the main entrance is via the wheelhouse. But not always; some welcome you at the bow.

A brief note on the material used in the conversion shell: the large majority are in steel, which provides flexibility of alteration and ease of maintenance and repair. Some wooden ones are found, but extra caution is needed to avoid rot and (often very hard to cure) roof leaks.

Think about windows. Beware the greenhouse look. You may want some wall space for pictures and cupboards. Seaworthy windows are well worth having, double-glazed and with heat-insulated frames if possible. These help avoid the potentially serious problem of condensation running off the glass in cooler weather and subsequent lining rot. Note whether the windows can be left ajar in the rain without getting your carpets wet (preferably not opening outwards, as this makes them very vulnerable to contact with waterway structures and other craft). Can they be securely locked shut if you go on open water or leave the craft unoccupied?

SYSTEMS

A barge needs all the systems of a house, and more. They tend to be more complex than domestic ones because they must usually be able to operate (at least for a while) independently from the municipal utilities. Beware: Some barges converted for strictly residential use do depend on shore hook-ups, and may have no independent systems at all. When they are untied from the bank, the power goes off, taps run dry and the phone goes dead!

Access to pipework and cabling is very important and beware of underfloor   pipework – that is where a hidden joint will leak one day. Ideally systems should be run above floor level – often up under the side-deck with suitable access or crawl spaces to sight, maintain and update them.

Water

Barge domestic water systems have several main components:
- One or more tanks
- One or more pressure pumps
- A method of heating water
- Distribution piping and fixtures.

Tanks are made from a range of materials. The best is probably stainless steel, but polypropylene (rigid plastic), plastic fabric (in a supporting box), fibreglass and mild steel are all acceptable. They must be leak-proof and have proper support (a full tank is heavy, and you do not want it to move if the barge rolls). They also should be symmetrical across the barge (so no list develops when water gets low), and accessible for cleaning and repairs. Larger ones need internal baffles to stop the contents surging about. Be sure to check they are not growing green crops inside (although these can be cleared up).

The total water storage volume you need depends on how much water you will use (how many people, bath or shower, summer or winter, etc.) and how long you will be forced to go between fills. Also, on how much of the barge's internal space you want to sacrifice to tankage (this applies to storing waste and fuel as well as water). Typically water tanks will be more than 1000litres.

Most water systems are pressurised, usually by an automatic electric pump with a pressure switch (although hand-pumping can still be found). The more expensive the pump, the higher the flow. Water pump noise can be intrusive, particularly at night, so pumps should be carefully located and sound-insulated.

Water heating is usually by a hot water tank. The tank can be heated by a calorifier coil using waste heat from the main engine or from a water-cooled generator (a very worthwhile arrangement for saving fuel), a (separate) calorifier coil from the central heating system, an electric element (if there is a connection to shore power, or a large generator), water heating solar panels or a combination of these. On demand gas burning boilers are still around but not popular as they have very specific regulatory requirements.

Piping is usually plastic with some copper. DIY piping systems are common but workmanship varies widely. Convenient valves at low points for draining the system, and bleeders at high points for removing air, are important. Insulation of the pipes is advisable.

Waste water removal

Waste water from barges is of two types: grey water (from sinks and baths) and sewage, or black water, (from toilets).

In most places it is legal to discharge grey water straight into whatever you are floating in. There are a couple of points to consider. Are the drains above or below the waterline? Above is safer and may be insisted on by your insurer. Are the fixtures (particularly the bath or shower) above water level or do they require a drain pump? Drain pumps on baths and showers are prone to corrosion and clogging with hair, so can have quite short lives unless fitted with effective hair traps. Whale gulper pumps have a good reputation for longevity even when pumping dog hair!

The traditional Dutch solution to sewage disposal was to mount the toilet on a large vertical pipe opening out through the bottom of the barge. Use of these, and other 'sea toilets', is illegal in UK inland waters and many other European countries. The approved answer is some form of holding tank which is emptied into shore sewer facilities.

Holding tanks are made of the same range of materials as water tanks, but the preference for stainless steel or polypropylene may be stronger here due to the rather more unpleasant consequences of leakage. Size of tank will again depend on the usage of the craft, and whether you use water-flush toilets. Other toilets vary from simple drop-through ones which mount on top of the tank (in the simplest case the tank is portable and carried to the disposal point) to macerator pump equipped conventional house toilets, to high-tech vacuum systems which minimise flushing water (sometimes canal water is drawn in by a separate pump for flush toilets).

Shore disposal facilities often include tank pump-out services for a fee, but you may wish to have your own pump to avoid these charges and for added flexibility. These need to be robust, quite high volume, and able to deal with water with a high solid content. With the right plumbing, they can double as emergency bilge pumps, bath draining pumps or for running a deck hose.

'Composting' toilets have become more popular in recent years. They are wrongly named. The toilet only separates liquids and solids. The liquid needs disposing of appropriately - Elsan disposal point - and the solids need composting. This involves on board tanks or a shore facility. UK authorities have recently banned disposal of solids in their refuse facilities.

Cinderella toilets are the latest solution. Solids are burnt and the liquids evaporated. They are power hungry, need a fan and large inlet and outlet ducts. Good solution if included in new-build or conversion but difficult to retrofit. The burn time is typically 40 minutes – not good at bedtime!

Electricity

Most barges have a DC electrical system, like a car or caravan. Some are 12 volt, but many are 24 volt. The latter system results in lower current for the same power and so can be built with wiring of smaller cross-section. 24 volt equipment is slightly less readily available (but many larger trucks and motorhomes use 24 volt, so it is not really a problem).

Such a system has a battery bank. The capacity of this is measured in amp-hours or kilowatt-hours, but you should not expect to make effective use of more than about half the stated capacity due to the physics of the ubiquitous lead-acid battery. Batteries more than five years old are suspect, and they are not cheap to replace. Check that there is a separate battery for starting the engine, as you would not want to be rendered immobile because someone ran down the domestic battery by falling asleep in front of the late movie on TV.

Battery development stalled for most of the last century but was kick-started by space travel research, solar power storage and the climate changing moves from fossil fuelled cars to electric propulsion. We won't try and cover this fast moving subject in this book as there are extensive discussions of both battery type and electric propulsion on the DBA Forum.

Batteries have to be recharged. The barge should have one or more means of doing this. The simplest is an alternator on the propulsion engine. This can work fine when the barge moves frequently (which really means daily for several hours). But even then the alternator must be powerful enough to charge the battery in that time. 100 amps for a 24 volt system is now a reasonable standard. The output of an alternator varies with how fast it is turning, so it is important that the engine pulley driving the alternator is big enough to ensure that the alternator is giving full power at normal cruising speeds.

However, a main engine alternator is not a good solution if the barge is likely to remain stationary, because long periods of running a large diesel with only the alternator for a load will shorten the engine's life significantly.

A mains-powered charger is useful for charging the batteries for when the barge is not moving. This requires a mooring with a shore power supply. Such a charger need not be large as it can conveniently be left running for long periods.

Solar panels are becoming popular means of charging batteries – barges have large decks/roof space. It is unlikely that solar alone will sustain your batteries if stationary in UK in winter but it is also common to hear of systems needing to dump electrical energy in the summer – especially in central Europe. Do note that the solar panels will need their own controller to manage the charge going into the batteries. Panels can vary in size from the small car battery panels used to maintain the starter battery when moored away from shore power to full deck area arrays that generate enough electricity or limited propulsion as well. This is another fast moving subject regularly discussed on the DBA Forums.

Wind generators are common on sea-going sailing yachts but not a good solution for barges which are often in areas of wind-shadow and as they need clear air they do need to be on a mast. Their main drawback is noise and vibration which is easily amplified by a steel barge deckhouse!

Most barges have an on-board generator, preferably diesel, coupled to a large charger. Petrol is legal on barges but not recommended due to the safety problems from its vapours entering the barge. On board generator engines can be either air or water-cooled. Air-cooled ones may be cheaper but are noisier, an important consideration to both you and your neighbours when you remember how long generators have to run. Also, you cannot use the waste heat from an air-cooled engine to warm your water, but instead have to vent the hot air to the outside. A generator usually runs at a fixed speed. The common speeds are 1,500/minute and 3,000/minute. Higher-powered generators usually run at the slower speed, which tends to be quieter and to let the engine last longer. Modern generators have a separate alternator to charge their own starter batteries.

With a generator, a more potent charger is merited to reduce recharging (and thus generator running) time. For 24 volt systems, 50 or 75 amps is a common rating, but 100 amps is better. Charger technology varies considerably and is evolving rapidly, and an older machine may not recharge a battery nearly as quickly as a new one with the same amperage rating.

Since the generator will almost always be 230 volts AC, it powers the charger and provides mains current to (a separate system of) wiring through the barge. This will enable you to use all your usual domestic equipment and appliances, which will be much cheaper than equivalent DC versions.

A charger requires 2kVa to 3kVa, and a washing machine or dishwasher 3kVa. So if you expect to use the normal range of domestic electrical equipment, you should look for a generator in the 6kVa to 10kVa range. Anything larger will probably be too lightly loaded for its own good, and waste space.

The 230V system will only be of use when the barge is plugged into the shore or the generator is running. Unless, that is, there is an inverter, a device which changes DC battery voltage to AC 230v house power. Most barges now have these. Ideally these should be a minimum of 3 kVa and 6kVa are common. Good large-output inverters are not cheap, but it may be possible to recoup their costs by the savings made by using 230V equipment. Several reputable brands are available, with Victron and Mastervolt probably at the forefront at present. Combined charger/inverter units are now common and on limited shore power can manage the draw from shore balancing it with draw from the batteries. It is, however, a potential single point of failure leaving you without AC 230v supply.

Without meaning to drag you into technicalities, we should point out that there are different forms of AC. Certain inverters produce electricity that some appliances, especially washing machines and dishwashers do not like. 'Square wave' is not as good as 'modified sine wave'. Full 'sine wave' is best (and, as is the way of the world, requires the most expensive equipment to produce).

More modern barge electrical systems often include one more piece of equipment which you may not have heard of: the isolation transformer. This is located between the electrical connection to the shore and the barge's on-board 230 volt wiring. Its purpose is to prevent stray electrical currents which can all too easily flow back to ground through the barge's hull and the water when you are plugged in to the mains, and which can in the worst cases cause the hull to corrode with quite frightening speed. One can always be added later, but they cost several hundred pounds. If there is not one, and the barge has been on the mains for most of the time, pay particular attention to the hull thicknesses on the survey report (discussed later).

You will also come across galvanic isolators which are fitted to offer protection from both stray currents & galvanic currents. Good quality ones will have a test facility to prove that they are working.

Wiring systems merit close inspection. There are limited national and no international standards. Many have been installed or altered by amateurs and can be death traps. A tidy installation, with well supported cabling clear of the bilges and with adequate circuit breakers, is the minimum to look for unless you are prepared for a lot of remedial work.
The wire itself must be multi-strand as opposed to single-core, as the latter can become brittle at terminals and snap over time due to vibration. (where safety regulations apply they all demand multi-strand).

Think about where and what electricity outlets you require, as it is not easy to add additional cables to a fully lined-out craft. Remember to consider the range of lighting you will need and preferably have a mix of DC 12/24v and AC 230v for redundancy when problems occur! The most efficient lamps are Light Emitting Diodes (LED) which are available to suit 12v and 24v systems (usually shown as 10-32v in catalogues) and also available for 230v systems.

Heating and Ventilation

There are as many types of heating system as there are preferences, from solid fuel stoves to sophisticated programmable diesel furnaces or boilers.

Solid fuel needs storage with easy loading access for the bulky coal or wood. Many people would not be without the cheerfulness of a real fire, and a lot of barges have them. But remember the drawbacks of ash and dust. One way of having your cake and (h)eating it is a hearth-effect diesel or gas burner.

Gas equipment (for space or water heating) is compact and needs little maintenance. However, bottled gas (propane is better than butane at low temperatures in cold weather) is a much more expensive fuel than oil per unit of heat. Also you have to keep changing those cumbersome bottles, and there are different types of bottles and connectors in different countries. Some safety authorities look unfavourably at some on-demand gas water heaters.

Diesel-burning hot-air or hot-water systems are increasingly popular. Many barges benefit from a constantly-burning heat source in cold weather. But for summer and autumn, the extra flexibility of a fire on demand programmable system, such as those made by Webasto, Mikuni, Bubble, Kabola and Eberspacher, are a bonus. They are more complex and require correspondingly more maintenance, and create a constant electrical drain. Diesel burning central heating boilers, as used ashore in houses, are also very common, are usually cheaper to buy and maintain, and can be run off the 240v inverter power supply. Some owners prefer to use kerosene or home heating oil as it is cheaper than red diesel. The disadvantage is the need for a separate tank and fuel system and much more restricted waterside availability in bulk.

Don't overlook the possibility of using the waste heat from the main engine or a water-cooled generator. By using a calorifier (heat exchange coil) in the hot water tank, you can provide all your hot water this way whenever the engine concerned is being run regularly.

As in a house, a comfortable barge should have a heat source in each room, including the wheelhouse. Make sure there are, or is room for, enough radiators and, especially in larger vessels, a suitable hot water circulating pump.

Ventilation is important. Fresh air is needed for breathing. Less obvious is the fact that people and domestic activities produce a lot of moisture which must be eliminated. Failure to do this will not only fog your windows, it will cause water to condense behind the cabin linings, leading to serious rot and other damage. Enough fixed vents at both high and low levels should be fitted in addition to windows (which you will want to keep closed in bad weather). This is now a requirement in the UK. Bilges also need ventilating to avoid rot in the floors.

Lining - Insulation

In the summer you will want your ship to stay cool inside; in winter you will want it to retain as much heat as possible. So insulation is a major consideration. It should be one of the first, too. It is often difficult to install or upgrade insulation after the interior finish is done.

Special fire-proof foam insulation sprayed on to clean dry steel work is easily the best way to insulate the top and sides. It must be applied professionally. Fibreglass or rock wool, battened to but slightly clear of the steel work and covered with a sealed heavy duty PVC moisture barrier, is a less effective alternative. Foil insulation such as YBS General Purpose Therma Wrap Insulation is becoming more widely used particularly for repairs and upgrading. Foam 5cm thick gives good insulation, fibreglass needs to be 7.5cm or 10cm thick and foil needs only to be 0.4cm thick for similar effectiveness. You will find polystyrene used but its flammability makes it a much less attractive material.

Every gap between the steel and internal linings should be filled with insulation, and sealed with a moisture barrier. Check carefully that this is the case, as otherwise you will get cold spots and (worse still) condensation in the walls no matter how well you ventilate.

Be careful to check that combustible material is not applied directly against the hull. This would be dangerous if you needed some repair welding.

Walls

Traditionally, lining is made of plywood, water-resistant or better, full marine quality. Waterproof MDF (medium density fibreboard) is also acceptable but not as good.

The best interior walls are a sandwich of two linings with the space between filled with wool insulation. They improve sound privacy and add a measure of fire retardance. Solid doors give a better feeling of quality than plywood. The sandwich can also be a route for both pipework and cables.

Ceilings can vary from wood planking to painted MDF. Walls can be finished in almost anything from paint to carpet.

The real decision for you, the purchaser, is whether you can stand the former owner's layout and taste and the quality of the work, or whether you will have to do minor or extensive refitting/redecorating. Yet again, this sort of work always seems to cost much more than it does in land accommodation.

Floors

Varnished planks, cork, and vinyl are easy care, but carpets can be vacuumed rather than swept or polished and are warmer in winter. Dutch families who used to work the barges insisted that outdoor shoes be removed before entering the living accommodation. After you have tracked large sections of towpath on to your nice pale rugs you may want to adopt this rule too (providing a supply of slippers of various sizes near the door can help your visitors go along with the idea).

However, one consideration the first-time buyer often overlooks (and this also applies to exterior walls below the water line) is that you may need access to the hull from the inside for repairs. A floor covered with carpet tiles can be easier to take up than one with wall-to-wall. Loose-lay vinyl is preferable to the glued-down variety. Smaller supporting or backing panels screwed into place allow quicker and easier access than do large sheets nailed down. Check how awkward it would be to take apart the interior structure in time of need.

Ballast

Perhaps this is not really a conversion item, but the topic fits here. Barges were designed to carry heavy weights, so they float high in the water when converted for leisure: sometimes too high, overall or at one end, for good manoeuvring or for getting under bridges. The solution is ballast, high density material usually installed under the floors.

Ideally, ballast should be removable so that the trim of the barge can be adjusted and so that you can get at the inside of the hull. Removable ballast might comprise steel or iron pieces, bricks, concrete blocks etc. But some barges are ballasted with concrete cast in place. This can be removed only by a jack-hammer, a very tedious job. It has advantages in strengthening the hull and protecting the interior from corrosion, but the French authorities disapprove of it because it is so hard to get out when a sunken vessel needs to be raised. Overall, this type of ballast must now be considered negatively, although a lot of barges have it.

Best practice demands a small air space, wooden or plastic battens, between the ballast and the hull, to allow ventilation and drainage and to prevent the ballast moving and damaging the hull plating.

Furniture

The vendor may not leave you much portable furniture, but there may be quite a bit built in. Are there enough cupboards and drawers of a suitable shape? Are the beds long enough, and spaces above the mattress high enough for normal people (people in the past were not as tall as nowadays)?

If you have some beloved furniture you intend to install, do not forget to check if you can get it on board. Barge doorways are seldom of standard domestic size. But maybe there is a large and removable skylight or hatch?

For any soft furniture, check that the foam or other filling meets current fire-retardant standards. Much does not, and these regulations are being enforced ever more toughly.

Too much free-standing furniture may not be a good idea. It can move alarmingly when the barge is in rough water.

Other

Varnished woodwork can be beautiful (although too much can make the world seem awfully brown). If it needs revarnishing, there might be a lot of work ahead. If the varnish has deteriorated near windows, the essential anti-ultra-violet type which resists the effects of sunlight may not have been used. Many people now opt for modern woodstain preservative treatments, especially for external wood work. It does not have the same high gloss but is much more user-friendly.

Domestic equipment

Any gadgets you have in your house, you can have in your barge. Let us start with the kitchen (or galley).

The overwhelming choice for barge cookers is bottled propane, because gas burners are instantly adjustable. Unfortunately propane is heavier than air and, if the system leaks, can collect very dangerously in the bilge. If there is any gas system on board, look for electronic gas detectors. You also find oil or solid fuel occasionally (Aga / Rayburn-type stoves are sometimes installed for cooking and excellent backgound heat). Electric cooking is possible but usually requires a generator to be kept running for anything more than two rings or an oven. The combination of a Rayburn for winter cooking and heating and two electric rings and a small oven for summer can work well (especially backed up by the BBQ!).

Lots of equipment can be installed in a well planned galley

Barge fridges can be gas but electric is the now the safe norm. 'Yachty' DC fridges are much more expensive than the conventional domestic AC fridges. Toasters, mixers, etc.? Almost exclusively AC, so now you see why inverters are ever more popular. Although a 2kW inverter can readily handle a fridge (given enough battery capacity), a dishwasher, washer, or dryer will need 3kW or more, and may better be run off a generator.

COSTS OF OWNERSHIP

Even if you never leave the mooring, the cost of barge ownership definitely does not end with the purchase cheque. Barges can be inexpensive homes, but do not underestimate costs such as moorings, licensing, regular docking and so on which defray the more obvious savings. We bring the main running costs to your attention below, to help you avoid getting in over your head (figuratively, of course).

NAVIGATION CHARGES

Inland navigations and harbours are governed by navigation authorities which levy a (usually) annual charge for keeping or using a craft on their waters. These charges vary substantially from authority to authority, both in magnitude and in how they are calculated.

Even the Environment Agency (EA), which manages navigation on a few UK rivers, does not have a uniform approach. On the non-tidal Thames, its charges vary with the length x beam of the craft. This number is multiplied by a standard charge/ m2/ year. So the owner of a 20m x 4m barge could be stuck with a bill of £1700 (2022) per year. However, on the non-tidal Medway, another EA river, the calculation is based only on length, and capped at 11m. The same craft would be charged £400 (2022) a year there.

Confusingly, the EA (like some other navigation authorities) sometimes refers to its navigation charges as 'Registration'. This should not be confused with the national shipping registry of the country concerned.

The Canal & River Trust (CRT), which controls most other river navigations and most canals in the UK, makes charges according to length, setting different rates depending on whether you want to use the rivers only, or the whole system. To use the River Lee navigation, for example, CRT might charge £700 per year (2022). To use the same barge on the canals as well, the fee would be about £1100 per year. However CRT are now applying a premium to wide boats (over 2.1 m) which will doubtless increase in future years.

To make things even more complex, EA charges for a 'houseboat' are half those for a cruiser; it defines a houseboat as one with no means of propulsion.

Each smaller navigation and harbour authority has its own charging scheme.

A final thought on navigation charges. If you venture off your home waters into those of another navigation authority, the other authority will require you to pay its charges for the time you are there, usually at a higher daily rate than you pay (pro-rated from annual charges) at home. You will not get a rebate from your home authority for time you are away. There are exceptions – if you pay your registration on the Medway or Thames then you are allowed to visit the 'other' waterway free of extra charge for two weeks.

CRT and EA have started some integration of their charges. The first result of this is the 'Gold Licence', which for an increased annual fee allows craft to use all the waters of both authorities.

In France things are a little different. They require each vessel to have a vignette, which can be bought for varying periods and for which the charge is based on length but is only required when moving.

Dutch waterways still tend to be free; Belgium makes a relatively nominal charge, but only in Flanders (€160 in 2022). Wallonia is free.

INSURANCE

All barges should be insured. This is not only
for your peace of mind; more and more navigation authorities and marinas insist on seeing proof of your, at least third party, insurance before they will let you on to their waters.

You will probably want three types of insurance cover: hull, third party liability, and contents.

Hull And Third Party Liability

It might be expected that insurance for big iron craft over 70 years old would be difficult and expensive to get.

The major problem was the unfamiliarity of UK insurers with the risks involved. This led to over-caution, and high premiums. However, one of the founders of the Association managed to arrange a scheme particularly for barges, and since then several other insurers have developed competing schemes.

Of course, Belgian and Dutch insurers knew all along that barges are reasonable insurance risks, being familiar with them and accustomed to vessels built in the 1890s still being in trade. Competitive premiums can be arranged for vessels based in the Netherlands. The obvious snag is the language problem. Policies are written in Dutch and governed by Dutch law. There is clearly a risk of misunderstandings, and potential difficulties in pursuing anything other than a straightforward claim.

The UK's departure from the EU has added some complexity and non UK and non EU owners will have some increased difficulty matching residence, boat location and registration with an appropriate insurer. Members' experiences and recommendations are in the Forum section of the DBA website. Haven Knox-Johnston have operations in both the UK and the EU and a members' application form is on the website along with details of other insurers who will cover barges.

Typical cover is for loss or damage to hull and major equipment, and against third party claims of up to £3,000,000 or more. The insured value is usually based on the purchase price or a professional valuation.

As a guide, with an excess (deductible from each claim) of £500, the annual premium for craft in UK inland waters (e.g. not below the Thames barrier) might be 1% of insured value.

Contents

If you will be living aboard, you will probably want insurance for your barge's contents. The cover for cruising, or for the residential use of the barge, is similar to the comprehensive insurance available to a householder, but also includes the risk of sinking. Extensions are available for personal possessions against all risks while you are away from your vessel. A typical annual premium is about 1% of the value of contents insured.

MOORING

Although your mind will be focused on finding the barge, we should warn you that finding a satisfactory mooring, especially if you want to live on it in Britain, may prove to be a problem. In fact, moorings deserve a publication all to themselves, and are somewhat beyond the scope of this handbook but there is an Annex on the website addressing the UK mooring issues.

The standard advice is 'Find your mooring before buying your barge' and we endorse this fully. However, it is fair to say that only a very small number of barge buyers follow this counsel!

In general, the situation is somewhat easier in other European countries than in Britain. Inexpensive short-term moorings can often be found in France, Belgium or the Netherlands but seldom in major cities even there.

Amenable permanent moorings can usually be found with some research, but usually at a higher price.

The trouble is that barges are somewhat larger than your average cruiser, so most moorings are not designed to cater for them. Some marinas welcome barges, others will be horrified.

An important point to note is that there is a very significant difference between a mooring for a vessel used principally for cruising and one for a residential craft. Setting up a new residential mooring is subject to local government approval, which is not easily obtained in most cases. Boats on approved residential moorings often sell for much higher prices than the worth of the boat just because of the mooring, even though the mooring may have no security of tenure. It is not uncommon for someone to buy a boat he does not want, just to get its mooring. However, if thinking of this, check that putting a different craft on the mooring is allowed. Surprisingly often it is not.

Your broker (if you buy through one) may be a good place to start looking for a mooring, but do not be too optimistic.

Your hunt for a mooring must concentrate on the local area in which you wish to keep your ship. Do a bit of towpath walking, visit other boat owners, and you will probably get direct information on what is or is not available.

Moorings may be available from the navigation authority for the waterway concerned, from commercial mooring operators (marinas, inland etc.), private riparian owners, and the secondary market (those who no longer need their moorings and wish to pass them on).

UK

The EA in UK operates moorings in lock approaches and weir streams and charges for stays. Most river moorings are privately owned or managed. The EA does, however, possess and exercise a considerable degree of control over where moorings can be established, and what they can be used for. Do not assume that the purchase of freehold riverbank implies an automatic mooring right. If you are considering a mooring on EA waters, verify carefully with the appropriate EA office that a mooring there is acceptable.

CRT in UK does administer some of the moorings on its system, but the majority are for non-residential craft only. For many years CRT had a policy of severely restricting residential moorings. Usually these were only available on a caretaker basis at boatyards. As a result, there developed a large number of 'continuous cruising' craft (technically boats without a home mooring) some of which in fact did not cruise at all. As a consequence, the chances of a newcomer finding an approved residential mooring were very slim in many CRT areas. However, the Trust has now changed its policies, and cares much less what you do on your moored boat provided you are at peace with your local government. The situation is not easy, but is somewhat better than it was.

There are many private moorings on both EA and CRT waters, from large basins to small lengths of bank. A few are residential, most strictly not, but some are in the grey area of unofficially residential. With these last you run the risk of suddenly finding that you may not live there any more as the result of some local government, NIMBY or landowner crackdown.

The Port of London Authority (PLA) controls mooring on the tidal Thames in UK (i.e. below Teddington in west London) and operates some pier and buoy moorings itself. Possibilities have been very limited on the tideway to date, but more recently a number of new sites have opened and more possibilities are in the pipeline. There are some established marinas, many in former commercial docks such as South Dock, St. Katharine's and Chelsea Harbour, which accommodate barges but are very expensive. CRT operates marinas in Limehouse and Poplar docks. Thistleworth Marina at Isleworth and the Hermitage Community Moorings downstream of Tower Bridge are examples of another more boater owned approach. These are moorings co-operatives in which you buy your mooring but the floating pontoons and services are managed jointly. There are also moorings, occasionally available long-term, on Chiswick, Cadogan and Dove piers. Tidal drying moorings are also available at various sites along the foreshore

The tidal Medway and Swale estuaries in Kent are rich in possibilities, with marinas such as those at Hoo and Medway Bridge Marina offering berths, and in numerous creeks and corners. In almost every case these moorings are drying, which means that your barge will sit on the mud, sometimes for most of the day, when the tide goes out. As they are tidal, you will be floating in salt water which is less kind to metal craft than is fresh.

The further from London, the easier mooring becomes. You do not have to be located in the Thames watershed.

Moorings are generally priced by length. As a guide, London Dockland moorings may go for £1500/ m/ year (2022), while a rural canal mooring well away from London might be less than one third of that. (Please remember that this is in addition to any navigation charges.)

Mainland Europe Moorings

In mainland Europe moorings are generally cheaper, except near the coast, where yacht mark-up applies, and in city centres especially in tourist destinations. Most marinas are commercially owned and charge market rates. Boat clubs often offer moorings at preferential rates if you join their club or association. In France the navigation authority VNF manages most of the linear moorings and are the authority to approach if you want to moor at the end of your property. Town moorings are usually managed by the Mairie. Belgium is very similar.

In the Netherlands, again the marinas are a mixture of commercial and boat clubs and in town centres moorings are usually charged for. Most towns offer some free short-term moorings near the boundary a short / long (!) walk into town. The The Marrekrite scheme, owned by 16 municipalities, operates in Friesland and manages a huge number of rural moorings. Facilities are usually limited to a regularly emptied rubbish bin and the usual time limit is 3 days – all for buying a 20 Euro pennant – see https://marrekrite.frl/varen

However, those charges may not be the whole story. You still have to consider utilities. Some moorings come with mains electricity and water, rubbish removal, good wifi, the ability to hook up a phone, parking and perhaps even a sewer connection, and include these in the price. Others may not have these services available at all; still others expect you to make your own arrangements and pay for each separately, and some may act as middleman and take a mark-up. In UK electricity has to be sold at cost but beware the heavily marked up monthly 'service charge' which is unregulated.

In general, utilities will cost you as much or more than they do for a house. If you generate your own electricity, it will certainly cost you more per kilowatt-hour than the local electricity company charges. The purchase price of your generator takes the place of the standing charge. You may find a mobile telephone is the only sensible, but often good, communications solution.

Finally, do not overlook local taxes. A barge is not real estate, but a mooring may be, and in the UK the local council tax (perhaps £1000 per year or more) can apply to residential moorings. The tax is usually assessed at the bottom band A rate but can be significantly higher if the mooring is freehold and/or in a desirable area.

MAINTENANCE

Like houses and cars, barges need regular maintenance. It certainly is not something to skimp on (not only will value decline, but it is much cheaper to keep a barge in good condition than it is to refurbish it later).

And, of course, you do not want your barge to sink, even at its moorings. The hull is most critical. This and underwater machinery, propeller, rudder, etc. are serviced when the barge is out of the water, in a dry dock or on a slipway or tidal grid. This should occur at least every four years as best practice although your insurer may only insist on every seven years after 30 years of age.

Docking can cost £200 to £300 per day, and you may need a week or more. While in dock, you will need a hull thickness survey (see the section on surveys later on) which may reveal some thin spots (anything less than 4mm) over which new plating must be welded. You will want the hull pressure-washed to get rid of growth, or perhaps even sand-blasted and repainted if corrosion is setting in, but be careful of blasting riveted hulls as it can undesirably loosen rivets and seams. While thinking of corrosion, you will likely need to replace the anodes, pieces of 'less noble' metal attached to the hull which, while corroding away themselves, prevent the hull from doing so.

Overall, a docking bill may reach thousands of pounds. No, you cannot put it off safely for very long!

Docking a barge in the Netherlands and Belgium is usually cheaper, and the required work tends to be done more cheaply and more efficiently than in Britain because they have more yards, there is more competition and they are used to dealing with larger craft.

The barge's topsides need regular attention too. A good exterior cleaning every month or so is a start. If you have the electricity supply to run it, a pressure washer is a good investment. Not only does this make the barge appear well cared for, but it also prevents grime standing on the paint and becoming a permanent stain. Repainting may be needed every four or five years, and varnished exterior woodwork needs redoing every two or three.

Barring breakdowns, propulsion machinery and the generator should need only normal preventive maintenance (oil and filter changes etc.). New batteries should be budgeted for about every five years. Domestic equipment and interior finishes require much the same attention as those in a house.

This section was not meant to scare you, but we do hope it has got rid of any impression that owning, or living on, a barge is a no-cost experience.

However, as a small ray of hope, there are ways to reduce some costs, for example by sharing certain services or patronising suppliers known for competitive prices or discounts to DBA members. See the Suppliers Directory in the Members' area of the DBA website.

THE SEARCH

THE MARKET

Barges, Brexit VAT and Visas

The departure of UK from the European Union on 31 January 2020 brought some unpleasant changes for barge owners. This is our understanding of the situation at February 2022.

Value Added Tax (VAT/TVA)

Good News - The taxation changes do not affect you if you buy and cruise in either the EU or UK and subsequently sell in the same customs area. VAT on sale and purchase of second hand boats is normally zero (with an exception for purchasing from a commercial undertaking).

Please note that Northern Ireland is a special case and currently (Feb 2022) very different regulations, duty and VAT apply. Please contact DBA – info@barges.org if you have queries relating to NI and barges.

Bad News - The first 'discovery' was that VAT is not just charged on first purchase, it is a transactional tax, and can come into play on every movement between the EU and 'third' countries. The transition period ended on 31 December 2020. That became the definitive date for VAT assessment. All ships in the EU retained EU Goods status and those in the UK became UK goods and after that date any ship moving between the EU and UK attracts VAT on its market value, and if by road on the cost of the delivery as well. Goods, which include ships and yachts, became subject to both VAT and Duty when exported. Duty is inconsequential at this point but could be invoked at a future date. VAT is 20% - 24% varying by country.

There are some relaxations.

The Temporary Admission (TA) procedure allows nationals of one state to take their ship abroad for 18 months and return without liability for VAT. This can be extended by taking the ship out of territorial waters (12 miles) and returning for another 18 months. Returned Goods Relief (RGR) allows freedom from VAT as long as the ship is in its original condition and still owned by the exporting owner for a period not exceeding 3 years.
Sailaway Scheme: See HMRC 703/2 – this allows non UK residents to take delivery of a new barge in UK without paying VAT and only paying

VAT on import to their country. The barge must be removed from UK within 6 months.

The UK government have temporarily lifted the 3 year limit on RGR for ships currently in the EU returning to the UK in the same ownership.

For ships entering the UK which are Qualifying Ships, as defined by HMRC 744C, the VAT rate is zero.

Certificates of Conformity

The EU Recreational Craft Directive was introduced in 1998 and all new build recreational boats between 2m and 24m had to be certified. All older vessels were exempt. When UK left the EU this was replaced with the UK Recreational Craft Regulations (RCR) which is currently (Feb 2022) identical. Any craft imported into UK will have to meet the RCR requirements. There is no exemption for older craft. The ship will need a "post construction assessment" that will require design data from which to calculate stability or that may be done by empirical testing. It will need details of other design features and equipment, including the engine, to show that it meets current standards. Not only is this process expensive (£5-8k) but an old boat is unlikely to meet the standards. This may change later in 2022 but do check sources such as the DBA website!

Crossing the Channel by barge

All movements between UK and EU are now subject to full reporting. Sadly neither the EU or UK have yet (Feb 2022) provided an electronic reporting system for recreational craft and reporting is by telephone or in person and may require a visit to a port with customs officials with full details of vessel and crew.

Prices, Choice and Selection

You are unlikely to buy a barge immediately usable for cruising or residence for less than £60,000, and that would probably be a small one. At that price, you would probably need to begin by spending more money on repairs or missing amenities. On the other hand, you could spend up to £1,000,000 buying and converting a 30m barge to a reasonable standard. In general terms, £160,000 might purchase a nice ship about 20m long, and £250,000 a very nice one (in 2022 prices).

The £160,000 barge might feel a better bargain than the £60,000 one, given all the equipment etc. that it comes with, which illustrates the point that it can be hard to get your money back if you do a luxury conversion.

Barges 17m–20m long by 3.5m–4.2m wide tend to attract premium prices. They have a wide cruising range, are of a manageable size to maintain and handle, fit many moorings and docks and generally do not require ESTRIN certification every 7 to 10 years (Criteria-20m or over length overall or Length x Beam x maximum Draft in m =100 or more)

Barges in the UK tend to sell for more than they do in the Netherlands. Many conversions in mainland Europe are of a lesser accommodation quality than those in the UK and the UK has more stringent safety rules and standards for equipment and installation for barges below 20m. But the selection is usually better in the Netherlands. If you are looking for an unconverted barge, the Netherlands is probably the best place to start. However, the few small barges (i.e. shorter than 30m) still in trade are mostly used for bunkering tankers or as crane ships, with a lot of equipment (tanks, etc.) which has to be removed before conversion can start. Most smaller barges on the market are conversions. If you can find one, a vessel still in trade can be a good buy. It will probably have had to be kept in good condition to do its work. But be cautious about the reason for sale, as the barge may have reached the point where keeping it in working trim is no longer economic.

Older conversions, particularly those used as houseboats deserve careful scrutiny. Hull maintenance may have been skimped, and the conversion may not meet current standards, especially with respect to gas and electricity systems. If they have been connected to the municipal utilities, their systems may not operate at all when they cast off.

WHERE TO LOOK

Our members' magazine, Blue Flag, always contains 'For Sale' advertisements from members and brokers. Our website www.barges.org has a 'For Sale' section and on the Links page of the site is a brokerage section with links to most leading brokers in Europe. Some UK estate agents offer barges and houseboats for sale, sometimes with moorings. Waterview and Waterside Properties are two of the leading agencies but moorings could crop up in any agency with waterfront properties.

Most of the European print publications have now been superseded by websites such as botengids.eu and apolloduck.com . Yacht and barge brokers now have comprehensive websites such as doevemakelaar.nl/en , h2ofrance.com , fikkers.nl, londontideway.com , bowcrest.com and dutchbargesforsale.co.uk

Your new barge may not look like much when you first see it

BROKERS

Many barge purchases involve brokers. There are a number of good ones and they can be very good value for money.

In Britain, a broker normally works for and is responsible to the vendor, not to you the purchaser. In the Netherlands, things can be different and a broker will happily work for the purchaser to find a suitable vessel (although unless you have agreed otherwise, he will be working for the vendor). He will either claim a finding commission if you buy something he has found for you, or charge a fee in advance for a number of introductions.

Practices vary, but it would be reasonable in negotiating any brokerage charges in advance to establish whether the broker is also being paid by the vendor.

Dutch brokers may advertise barges, and be able to source barges from other brokers. Dutch practice is that potential buyers deal with one broker only, who will if necessary offer barges from other brokers, sharing their commission by agreement. If you contact a number of brokers and they find they are all separately looking for the same barge for the same client, they will not be happy.

Brokers are less common in France, and in fact barge sales there are often more like those of houses and often do not involve a survey (as a result of stringent French laws on misrepresentation). However, these may not be much comfort to you when you are in another country, so insist on a survey even in France.

Not all brokers have the same idea of what constitutes appropriate business ethics. Before you sign up with one, ask around. Other barge owners are often very willing to talk about good, bad and legendary experiences with individual brokers. There are broker associations, which set standards for their members, in most countries where you might be buying. It can be worth asking the broker you are talking to which one(s) they belong to.

REPLICA / NEW BARGES

The new-build barge market has grown over the last 20 years. Many of these fabricators are UK-based and have their origins in narrowboat building, but there are Dutch and other European barge builders too. Some of the more recent designs of barges are beginning to resemble the elegant original lines of century-old Dutch barges, but using modern-day technology in design and construction. Many barges are CAD-designed and fabricated with steel cut with modern high precision laser/plasma cutters. Each 'jigsaw' piece is marked and welded together in sequence to form the barge hull and superstructure.

BARGE TYPE

The lowest cost barges are designed for predominantly canal use in the UK, and have a strong resemblance to narrowboat design. They are flat-bottomed, shallow draft, with skin-tank, water-cooled diesel engines suitable for sustaining the 4 knots maximum speed of UK canals. They are often called wide-beam boats or canal barges. Lengths vary between 12 and 20 metres.

Mid-market barges are generally squarer, having straighter lines (fewer curves) than top-end-of-market designs, but generally come complete with an enclosed wheelhouse. Most mid-market barges will be RCD Category D or C, and are often referred to as Dutch-style barges or river barges.

At the top end of the market, the barges are designed more for continental cruising along rivers with fairly frequent crossings of the English Channel etc. They have a more rounded shape, reserve buoyancy, a flowing sheer, a more powerful diesel engine (possibly riverwater cooled), rounded or angled chines (sides) for improved handling through the water, an enclosed wheelhouse which is likely to be collapsible for low bridges, though newer designs are increasingly using fixed wheelhouses with air draft of under 3 meters which will pass through the majority of European bridges and a deeper draft and probably more ballast / weight. Generally, the longer and wider the barge, the more aligned to continental cruising it becomes, although, to some extent, smaller barges do have a place in France where a number of marinas only welcome craft shorter than 15 metres. Be aware that different sets of rules can apply depending on boat length, typically in the ranges <15, 15 to 20 and >20 metres, the rules can also vary from country to country, so ensure that your chosen length will comply with rules for you chosen cruising areas.

Whatever the exterior design, the interiors can be modern or traditional design, basic or flamboyant, dark or bright. Most barge interiors are more house aligned than traditional boats. Some barge builders have fairly set design interiors, others are very flexible and will accommodate your own desires. Initially you may think you want your own interior design, but care must be taken to ensure that your design requirements are correctly interpreted by the builder, who must then guide his employees. Increasingly, new boats are becoming more power hungry, some using electric cooking for example, so ensure that your electrical systems can cope with your requirements. If you choose a builder that has a fairly set design, and have seen some of the company's previous builds, you will know how it will look. It may be wise to not vary too much from a builder's standard specification, they will be good at what they do often, but may struggle with systems etc. with which they are unfamiliar. Whatever you settle on as your specification, ensure it is included as part of your contract in case of any disputes at a later stage.

If you choose to new build, before making a decision on your builder, visit as many boats as you can, which have been built by them. It is a good sign when a builder puts you in touch with existing customers without them being present. When you finally select your builder, again try to visit as many of their existing boats and customers as possible to help you decide upon your final specification.

During construction, if possible, visit the builder as much as possible, particularly in the 'fit out' stages as it's much easier to correct something that you're not happy with before works progress too far. You may wish to employ a surveyor to inspect the boat at various build stages to ensure all relevant standards & specifications are being complied with.

When you take delivery of your new boat, ensure that you thoroughly test all of the systems and equipment at an early stage, it's much easier to address warranty issues before the boat is moved from the UK to France for example.

RECREATIONAL CRAFT DIRECTIVE (RCD)

Since 1998 all new barges built in Europe have had to comply with the Recreational Craft Directive (RCD) and to be marked with an individual CE identification plate which includes the category and maximum load and a Craft Identification Number. The builder will also have to provide an owners manual – ask to see it!

Within this directive are four design categories:

A, B, C and D. The lowest cost barges, designed mainly for canal use in the UK, will likely be Category D. Many new built replica Dutch barges are built to RCD Category C which is deemed suitable for wind speeds up to force 6 and significant wave height to 2m. A few barges are designed and built to Category B requirements.

A number of new barges, even with a C categorization, have a 'plumb' upright stem without much reserve buoyancy to minimize pitching fore to aft in any roughish weather. It is generally recognized that a forward-raking cone-shaped bow which flares outwards and upwards to the deck, thereby increasing the buoyancy in the bow area as the boat tries to pitch, is better for sea work. This sort of bow is seen on a coaster.

When selling a new unfinished barge (e.g. shell or sailaway), the builder must still categorise the boat, up to supplied level of build. Therefore you can buy a sailaway barge that conforms to RCD Category 'B, C or D' requirements. But because it is unfinished, a full conformation certificate cannot be issued: a Category C barge, for example, must take into account the electrical installation, gas installation, navigation lights, waste water discharge and have suitable fire extinguishers on board (none of which is likely to be supplied with an unfinished barge). Any buyer should therefore ensure that the 'sailaway' is supplied with an Annex III Declaration of Conformity (for partially completed craft). Many sailaways are DIY-completed by their owners, and never get a full RCD. This is allowable providing it is not re-sold within five years. Most insurance companies do not require any structural survey on a newbuild until it is 20 years old. If the sailaway is to be fitted out within the UK on a canal or non-tidal river covered by the BSS (Boat Safety Scheme) the Annex III document will be sufficient for the first year, and possibly longer if the boat is fitted out in accordance with the RCD regulations.

It should be borne in mind that the main thrust of the RCD is to ensure the boat meets the Essential Safety Requirements. This is different from judging how good a particular boat is at sea. So there is more to it than just whether your boat is a D, C or B category.

ESSENTIAL SAFETY REQUIREMENTS FOR DESIGN AND CONSTRUCTION OF RECREATIONAL CRAFT - 1. BOAT DESIGN CATEGORIES

Design category	Wind speed	Wave height	Comments
A Ocean	Beaufort 8+	4+ m	No barges to this spec.
B Offshore	< force 8 incl.	<4 m incl.	Few replica Dutch barges built to this spec.
C Inshore	<force 6 incl.	< 2 m incl.	Most Replica Dutch Barges built to this category
D Sheltered waters	<force 4 incl.	< 0.5 m	All narrowboats & most low- cost wide-beam barges

BARGE COMPLETION LEVELS

Most new-build barges are fabricated specifically to customers requirements. Many fabricators have a build-slot waiting list of around one year, so you will need to know your requirements in advance. Many fabricators are not canal side, so delivery is often by truck, at customer's expense, together with crane-in at destination.

Fully-fitted barge costs vary considerably. The lowest priced will be wide-beam barges that have the same lines as a narrowboat; they will have open tiller steering with no wheelhouse and probably large front-opening doors, and will be built to RCD Category D. These start from around £80,000 fully complete, although it is unlikely that any reputable builder will, these days, supply a full-fitted wide-beam for that price. At the top end of the market you could pay well over £500,000. A fully completed 55ft barge will almost certainly cost between £150,000 and £350,000 depending on shell type, engine and equipment specified. But you should be able to get a good fully fitted 55ft replica Dutch barge with collapsible wheelhouse build to RCD Category C for less than £300,000 with a reasonable level of equipment. These guide prices (2022) do not include VAT.

Around half of new-build barges built are delivered as 'sailaways'. A sail-away is a partly completed boat, ready to be craned into the water and steered under its own power to suitable moorings ready for completion. A delivered sailaway will be fully functional in that you will be able to cruise up and down rivers and canals at your leisure, but the inside will be totally empty. Think of it as a powered but empty snail shell, ready for spartan occupation. which you can use immediately.

A 'sailaway' generally comprises:

- Steel shell, complete with deck and cabins
- Cabin floor
- Working engine and steering
- Windows and external doors (sufficient to make the barge water-tight and secure)
- Steel fluid storage tanks for; diesel, drinking water and black (toilet) water
- Single coat of primer paint.

Some popular extras worth considering (making a sailaway-plus) are:

- Collapsible wheel house
- Internal wood battens and spray foamed insulation
- Large double-glazed roof hatch (around 5ft x 3ft) for getting
- furniture on board
- Bow and stern escape or 'houdini'-type hatches (you must provide an alternative escape route, otherwise the only way out is through the wheelhouse, under which is the engine which is a possible cause of fire)
- Extra coats of paint
- Bow-thruster tube (worth having fitted, as you can add the bow-thruster
- at a later date if / when required, without having the hull being cut and welded under the water line)
- More powerful engine (especially if it may be used along tidal rivers)
- Double glazed windows / port holes (in lieu of single glazed)
- Extra storage tanks for diesel and grey water
- Stainless steel fluid-storage tanks
- Full or partial internal lining

But there are no specific, standard specifications, so it is important to establish exactly what you are getting prior to placing an order. Once you have your sailaway barge, selecting appropriate equipment and fitting it out is very similar, if not exactly the same, as an original barge.

Completing the fit-out yourself will likely reduce costs considerably, but it is time consuming and some barges remain unfinished for three years, and more, after delivery! For a complete fit-out you must allow around 2,000 hours work; a sailaway with a few options should need fewer hours. One thousand hours of work equates to a year's weekends plus bank holidays, or two-and-a-half-days per week. But for each day working you will need to allow time for planning and preparation as well. A lot of reading will be required beforehand to familiarise yourself with specialist equipment installations; this can be done in the evenings. Typically, when fitting out a barge, for each day spent working on the boat, you should allow another six hours during the week (evenings) in preparation, planning and buying materials needed for the weekend.

Many barge fabricators will supply a shell only, but this is not so popular amongst buyers. The shell will rust very quickly without protection against the elements. A buyer will need to have a suitable, and preferably covered, location to complete the boat.

A number of companies will design a barge for you, enabling you either to fabricate it yourself, or get your favourite fabricator to build it for you. Some designers also have 'off the shelf' standard designs for sale. These are computer-originated CAD designs, from which the steel can be directly cut using modern high precision laser / plasma cutters. The 'jigsaw' pieces can then be sent directly to you or your chosen fabricator.

VIEWING

So you are still eager to be a barge owner. You are itching to go and look at some craft. But what will you look out for? This section is to help you with the first 'kick-the-tyres' inspection which you may be doing on your own, and which should enable you to weed out obvious duds early on.

INSPECTING A BARGE

We suggest you go through something like the following examination. We have listed the crucial things first, so you can soon stop wasting time on a clearly unsuitable vessel.

Always take notes and photos! Apart from the need to remember anything which worries you or which you want to question, you will find that the barges you see will tend to run together in your mind if you do not keep a record of each. You do not need to try to memorise this section before you head for the boatyard: just photocopy the check list in the Appendix or download it from the website Library.

Hull And Top

The first thing to check is whether the ship as a whole is any use to you. Is it a type you would be happy with? Does it (or can it be made to) sail, if that is what you want? Is it the right size (do not take the owner's word for this, but get out your tape measure)?

We assume you want a craft that is basically sound and will not need too much remedial work. Stand back and take a look at the hull. Is it straight? If it is significantly dented or knocked about, this may indicate a hard working life, but it could merely be evidence of a previous owner with weak steering skills. Apart from aesthetics, dents and knocks can be a problem because they may have provided locations for corrosion to start. Failure to have had dents repaired may also indicate a less-than-caring attitude on the part of a previous owner; this may show up in slackness elsewhere in the vessel. Can you see signs of pitting or corrosion along the water line, which may indicate extensive over-plating will be needed?

What does the conversion look like? Is it aesthetic, or clumsy? Does it make good use of the hull, or is it wasteful? Can you get around outside easily when on board, and have you room to tend ropes etc.?

What is the top made of? Does it have any obvious flaws (look particularly closely if it is wooden)? What types of windows does it have?

Have a look at the inside of the plating. There should be ways of doing this, perhaps by unscrewing wall or floor panels. Do you see rust? Not good, unless it is very minor. The inside of the hull should be protected from rusting with paint or, preferably, a coating of special Dutch hull grease! The space between the lining and the hull will often be moist, no place to allow rust to establish a hold.

Is there water in the bilge? Most barges leak a little through the stern gland, so a small amount of water inside, at the stern, is not necessarily a sign of trouble. However, if there are signs that there has been a lot recently, or if an automatic bilge pump comes on while you are on board (particularly if it comes on twice!), you probably should be concerned about how the water is getting in. While down there, check the type of ballast, and how it has been installed – again hull grease protection and some wooden or plastic battens to protect the hull from the solid ballast.

Interior

What is the first general impression of the interior? Is it clean and well maintained, or scruffy? If the latter, is it just dirt, or long-term neglect which will be expensive to remedy? Remember, bringing a barge back into condition can involve a great deal of work, and you may not want to tackle redoing all the interior finishes.

Take a sniff. Can you smell damp, or worse, mildew? If so, find its source. It could be a small roof leak, or some bad windows, but it could be inadequate overall ventilation which may have allowed condensation to start rot in several places. If you smell furniture polish and coffee or fresh baking, be pleased – but also cautious, as you may be in the hands of a good sales-man. How, and how well, is the barge insulated? Do the windows (or below them) show signs of condensation?

Is the overall layout both sensible and suitable for your purposes? Does it have enough of the right types of room? Will it sleep enough people? Is there enough headroom? Can shortcomings be fixed without too much effort?

What fitted furniture is there? What loose furniture will come with it? Can you get your furniture in?

Does the domestic equipment it comes with suit you? You can usually replace this later, but that will be another cost. Does it have other features you particularly want (a solid fuel stove, for example)?

Engine Room

Go into the engine room. What is your first impression? Is it easy to get into? Is all the machinery readily reachable? Are you sufficiently protected from the dangerous bits? If it is grubby and untidy, take note. It should not smell of diesel!

What type of engine and drive does it have? Is this what you want?

Are there signs of fluid leaks (not just damp, look for vertical rust streaks too) or temporary repairs?

Make sure all pipes and cables are properly secured to the hull or the engine, that the rubber fittings are not perished and that the jubilee clips (metal bands which clamp the ends of hoses in place) still allow opening and fastening.

Check the water in the engine header tank. If it looks murky, greasy, or white this could indicate a problem with the cylinder head gasket or the cylinder head itself. Check there is sufficient antifreeze in the cooling water (you need a special tester for this – inexpensive and you may already have one for your car). If not, the engine might have frost damage from a previous cold winter.

Look at the fuel tanks (often in the engine room). Are they in good condition? Are they big enough?

Is the exhaust wet or dry? If it is dry, the muffler and the exhaust pipes should be well lagged. How is the engine cooled?
Ask for the engine to be started. Does it fire up without problem?
Does it smoke (let it warm up before deciding as most diesels smoke and rattle when cold)? Does it make strange noises?

If the vendor does not want to take the barge out for a short trip (not necessarily an unreasonable position), ask him to run the drive at the mooring in forward and reverse at no less than 1000 engine rpm. (Check first that the barge is securely moored and that the propeller wash will not carry away any other boats, waterfowl nests, etc.). Any problems going into gear? Any nasty noises or vibration?

When the engine has been turned off, go back into the engine room. Any signs of distress (leaks, smoke, strange smells)?

Always ask to see the log when evaluating the engine. A conscientious owner will have kept a detailed record of engine maintenance and repairs, which can tell a very meaningful tale. No log? Be a little suspicious of any claims made concerning rebuilds, etc..

No matter what engine you find in a barge which appeals to you (this applies to other major equipment on board too, particularly the transmission), it is worth checking on the supply of parts, including whether they are (still) available at all for this make and model, and whether the distributors are conveniently located (considering your own cruising plans)

Systems

Get the vendor to describe each system to you in turn. If the person on hand cannot do that, ask him to find you someone who can. If no one can, be worried (who has been doing the maintenance?).

Look at each system in turn. Is the wiring/piping tidy, in good materials, properly supported, and (gas and electricity) not in the bilge?

Regarding the electrical systems: are there adequate and accessible circuit breakers (or fuses, not uncommon in older installations) with labels? Are batteries accessible, full of electrolyte, and free of salts on the terminals? When were they installed? What is the capacity, type and age of the batteries, inverter, generator? Does the generator start easily, sound healthy, and not smoke?

Try every light and appliance, and get clear explanations of anything which is not working. Turn on a couple of heavy electrical loads at once for a few minutes (if the system is intended to stand it) and see if any circuits trip.

Be suspicious if any of these tests fails.

Look at the domestic water pump, and listen to it run. Is the flow adequate from the taps, particularly with more than one on? Look at the water tank. Is it in good condition externally? Is the water inside clean? Is it big enough?

How is the sewage handled? Is the holding tank big enough? What is it made of, and what is its condition? Is there a discharge pump, and is it working properly?

How is the barge heated? Ask for the heating to be fired up, even in summer, and check that the circulation system is functional. Is there adequate ventilation to the boiler?

Check for all required safety and navigation equipment. Do the lights, horn, radio, AIS, GPS, radar etc. all work?

What type of steering is installed? Does the system look well maintained (i.e. are cables greased and taut, are there signs of leaking hydraulic fluid)?

DOCUMENTS

Ask to see the ship's papers. You should look for the following.

PROOF OF OWNERSHIP

Proof of ownership varies from country to country and will need to be checked fully if the purchase proceeds. For now, just ask to see whatever proof there is. If nothing can be produced, or if it looks unconvincing, or if it is in names you do not recognise, ask questions.

DESCRIPTION

Many vessels have some form of measuring document. In the Netherlands, all trading barges had to have the Meetbrief. Even an out-of-date one is useful for verifying dimensions. It will also tell you the original registration code of the barge, which is helpful if you want to track down its history. If this code contains a 'B', as most do, it means the barge was built for Binnen (inland) use, and so is probably not suitable for extensive cruising at sea.

SURVEYS

You will (no exceptions, please!) need to get any craft you are serious about surveyed by your own surveyor before completing purchase to ensure your own protection – only the person commissioning the survey has any comeback on the surveyor. But start by asking to see any reports of previous surveys. When was the survey done and why? What was the hull thickness (there should be a plan showing the thickness found at each testing point)? What problems were found by the surveyor, and can the vendor show that they were properly remedied?

Be careful here. Just because a barge has been surveyed does not mean that it has passed any tests of acceptability. A survey is not a guarantee of good condition; it is simply an inspection by an expert. The survey may have found the barge to be in terrible shape.

Remember – Caveat Emptor applies – the seller does not have to declare any deficiencies but they must answer any question accurately.

CERTIFICATES

Many national jurisdictions and navigation authorities require craft to be inspected periodically for safety etc. Ask to see any certificates that the barge has. Are they current? If not, why not? If the length is over 20m overall or the length x beam x certified maximum draft in metres is over 100 then the ship will require a European Certificate (TRIWV, ES-TRIN) for use on mainland European inland waterways. (UK has not signed up to this requirement). In UK a Boat Safety Certificate is required on canals and most rivers. Newer boats built under RCD rules will need certifying under EU or UK rules depending on where they are lying.

LOGS

Not every barge owner keeps a log of any kind. But many do, not only of cruises but also of maintenance. Ask to see any that are available.

Has much work been done? Are there any recurring problems? Have reputable traders been used? Are the bills available to substantiate log entries?

Your investigations may be hampered by language difficulties, or simply by a desire not to intrude and appear too suspicious in the presence of congenial owner-occupiers. The results should still be valuable, though. Again remember – Caveat Emptor applies – the seller does not have to declare any deficiencies but they must answer any question accurately.

Even if you are no expert, at the end of the inquisition you should be able to form a reasonable idea of the overall condition of the barge. Problems of condition do not, of course, rule out a purchase, as the barge may be one you particularly like. But at least you will be going ahead with your eyes open wider and perhaps be better able to compare this barge with others and to consider the reasonableness of the asking price.

Keep your notes safe. Otherwise you will soon be confused as to which barge was the one with thin stern plates and which had a leaking fuel tank.

THE PURCHASE TRANSACTION

You have flown to the Netherlands several times. You have slogged around a slew of boatyards, always in the rain it seems. You have looked at rust buckets (just about floating, thanks to pumps), vessels with conversions that defy all logic or aesthetics, and beautiful ships beyond the budget of your dreams. But finally, just the right barge has appeared. You have decided to take the plunge. But how?

Like any financial transaction, a barge purchase can be handled in many ways. We will describe what we think is good practice, but there may be sound reasons for variation in particular cases.

A lot of money is about to change hands, so formality and attention to detail are vital. Do not get rushed by fear of losing the deal. Do not accept unsubstantiated statements about important matters. Remember, while you have got the money, you are in the driver's (helmsman's?) seat.

There are two ways you might proceed. One is to make the offer fairly general and 'subject to contract', and negotiate detailed terms of the purchase after you have an indication from the vendor that your offer may be acceptable. The other is to make the offer so complete that it is effectively a contract itself once a few blanks (particularly the vendor's name and signature!) are filled in. The latter has many appeals. It can speed up negotiation and processing in general, and it can help prevent the seller accepting a higher offer. We will assume this is the route you will follow, but if you do not, items which we suggest but which you leave out of the offer should probably appear in the final contract.

Beware, though. If you do make the offer quite complete, it is likely to become a binding agreement if the vendor accepts it in full and signs it. That is a major strength of this approach. But it means that you should be sure your offer is serious. You might otherwise find you are buying a barge when you thought you were merely testing the water.

We cover the purchase process assuming you will go through the following steps: offer, acceptance, survey, completion. We also suggest how you might get some professional help if you need it.

THE OFFER

To get things off to a firm start, you should make an offer to purchase, and we suggest you make it as clear and complete as possible (and in writing).

PUT IT IN WRITING

The offer should definitely be in writing, with your witnessed signature and the date. This does several things for you. It makes it clear that an offer has actually been made. It establishes when it was made, which can help prevent delays in presenting it to the owner by, for example, an agent who would like to solicit and present an alternative offer first. It shows you are serious. It makes it less likely that the terms of your offer will be misunderstood.

On this last point, by all means write up your offer in English, no matter in which country the barge is being sold. You may find yourself much better off if the offer (and contract, if there is one) is in your language. If you are working with a broker, he will be able to translate it for the vendor if necessary. Even if you aren't, almost any vendor in Europe will know someone who can do so. But do make sure that the vendor gets a copy of the original along with any translation, and that you get a copy of the translation.

The broker may provide you with a 'standard' offer or contract form in a language other than English. Unless you speak that language fluently and are qualified as a shipping lawyer do not sign any such document without an English translation. If you do get a contract in English scrutinise it very carefully. For example, contracts have been submitted which, at first sight, appear to make a purchase subject to satisfactory survey but, on close examination, allow a buyer to reject a barge after survey only for defects which arose after the buyer inspected the barge himself.

If you are given a contract in English, and are asked to sign it before your survey, read it very carefully. If anything looks dubious, it probably is. The best advice is not to sign any contract until you are completely satisfied.

You may be told that, for example, the Dutch do business on an oral contract and a handshake. It is not clear how legally binding this may be. It might be better to avoid formal handshakes! You may also be told that the sellers do not do this or that, often when you are being asked to do something against your better judgement. If it is against your better judgement, ask for an explanation and if you are still in doubt do not go along with it.

WHAT ARE YOU BUYING?

The offer should identify as exactly as possible the barge you are offering to buy. Refer to a registration number if possible. Otherwise, describe the vessel and where and when you saw it in enough detail to avoid any possibility of mistaken identity (or even substitution).

Specify an inventory of what you expect to come with the barge in the way of equipment, furniture, etc.. You do not want to show up on acceptance day to find that there is no longer a dinghy to take you to the mooring buoy and, when you get there, that the sophisticated radio system has vanished.

Whom are you buying from?

Those who claim to be owners do not always turn out to be so. It is prudent to make sure who owns the barge you hope to buy.

Direct contact with the owner can help. Meet him on his barge if possible, to satisfy yourself and to build a working relationship with him. Once you've met him, keep him informed of any bid you make and what you are doing. Do not just tell the broker. 'Misunderstandings' have been known to arise.

However, it can often prove quite legitimately impossible to get in touch with the owner. He may be out of the country, or simply wish his broker to handle the whole thing. In this case, you might ask the broker to state in writing the identity of the owner. You may also wish to see evidence that the broker is authorised to act for the owner, and in particular to accept purchase deposits.

WHAT ARE YOU PAYING?

Set out exactly what payment you are offering in total, and in what currency. Detail when the payment would be made. Do you want to make payment in three stages? Say so, and how. Do you have to get the money out of a term deposit in the Cayman Islands and have it changed into euros? Make sure you leave yourself enough time to do this, preferably stated relative to some clear event in the process.

Remember, the amount you propose and all the conditions constitute an offer. By all means pitch it as far below the asking price as you think you can get away with, but expect to negotiate.

Don't forget taxes. EU countries all have Value Added Tax (VAT), a form of sales tax. Rates vary from country to country, but it is always significant (in the UK it is 20%), If you are buying from an individual (even one represented by a broker), this tax does not apply. But if you are buying from a (VAT-registered) business, it often does. Be sure to confirm the VAT status of the vendor.

In the UK, the rate of VAT is 0% (yes, zero) if the vessel being purchased from a VAT-registered business is a 'qualifying ship'. As UK HMRC says, a qualifying ship is 'A vessel of a gross tonnage of not less than 15 tons which is neither designed nor adapted for use for recreation or pleasure'. A case in the 1990s confirmed that residence is not recreation or pleasure, so if you are buying the barge designed to be lived on you may be able to avoid paying VAT. However, this applies only in the UK. There is no such zero-rating for barges in other EU countries. However, if your purchase in the Netherlands is a new barge you intend to take to Britain to live in, it is possible to recoup the tax in certain circumstances.

VAT is a complex topic. If you think you may be facing it, seek some professional advice (or contact the DBA).

You should expect to put down a deposit right away if your offer is accepted. Say how much you are proposing (10% may be reasonable), who will hold it, and what happens to it – both if the purchase goes to completion and if it does not. Take this into account in your payment terms. Be careful to get a written receipt for your deposit, preferably in English, which leaves no doubt what the deposit is for.
Make it clear who will pay each broker involved, and when.

WHAT'S THE DEAL?

You will not be proposing just to put down your money and cruise away. There will always be other conditions you will want met. All of these should be set out in the offer.

SURVEY

One condition should always be 'Subject to survey and the vessel being in an insurable condition'. You should set out your right to have a suitable survey done by someone of your choice, and also the timing for getting the survey done (including the vendor making the barge available at an appropriate location), who pays for it, and what happens as a result of it.

Because this is so vital, we go into it in more detail later.

Usual practice is for the purchaser to pay for the survey and docking or slipping needed to carry it out.

TITLE

Title to the vessel, and the right of the vendor to sell it, should be satisfactorily substantiated. All liens and other claims on the vessel must be cleared, and warranted to have been cleared, by the vendor as part of completion.

You should require that title be transferred to you as part of completion. It can be a good idea to set timing for this. You should insist on provision by the vendor of a properly signed bill of sale.

REGISTRATION

The barge may be on a register when you see it. You may need to have it removed from that register, or instruct that it be re-registered in your name. If so, you should make timely execution by the vendor of the documents necessary to do this a condition of the offer.

OTHER

You may require other points to be confirmed, for example, that the vessel's size falls within certain specified dimensions, if this is crucial to you. This can be confirmed during the survey.

OBLIGATIONS

Specify what happens after acceptance. Who has to do what by when? If something is not done on time, do you or the vendor have the right to break things off? What happens then to the deposit? Must the vendor reimburse your expenses if he cries off?

The usual arrangements are as follows. If you withdraw arbitrarily (i.e. for a reason other than covered by a condition in the offer) or fail to complete in time, the vendor can cancel the contract and keep both your deposit and his barge. If he withdraws arbitrarily or fails to complete, you can cancel the contract and he should pay all your expenses of docking and surveying and a further set sum or percentage to offset your legal or notary fees and travel expenses, your wasted time, and the possibility that you missed buying another barge in the meantime.

KEEP IT SHORT

The document should state how long the offer remains open. A few days should be enough in most cases.

THE DOTTED LINE

It should have a space for the vendor to sign his acceptance and for his signature to be dated and witnessed. It should require that the signed document be delivered to you at a specified address within a specified short time of signing.

ASSISTANCE

If you feel all this is a bit out of your depth, get professional help. In the UK, it could be a lawyer (but finding one familiar with buying barges in mainland Europe is quite a trick). In the Netherlands, you can use a notary who (for a few hundred Euros, of course) will help you draw up the documents (offer and/or contract), do title and lien searches, execute the ownership transfer, and handle registration. Dutch notaries are professionally independent, so it is all right to use one suggested by the vendor's broker.

If you would like to avoid professional fees, obtain a copy of the sample Agreement for the Sale and Purchase of a Second-Hand Vessel published by the British Marine Industries Federation (BMIF). This may not exactly fit your case, but can be a useful guide to wording your own document. BMIF normally provides these to its members only, so you may need to ask a UK boatyard or chandler to get one for you.

ACCEPTANCE

Your initial offer will quite likely be rejected. The vendor may not like your price, or may not be willing to go along with one or more of your conditions. If this is the case, try to get him to make you a counter-offer; in effect, to say he will accept your offer if certain points are changed. The advantage of this is that it allows all the non-contentious points in your offer to be accepted and put to one side. Any further negotiations can focus on the key issues.

With luck, after haggling, you will arrive at an agreement. As soon as this is signed by the vendor, and any amendments initialled by you, the clock starts to run again – you must organise the survey and perhaps financing.

THE SURVEY

WHY YOU HAVE TO HAVE ONE

There is no question. The vessel must be surveyed afresh by a surveyor of your choice before purchase. Do not accept as sufficient a survey report produced by the owner or broker, no matter how recent.

It should be obvious that you need a survey for your own protection, but there is a second reason. You probably will not get insurance cover without presenting a survey report drawn up by a surveyor with acceptable qualifications including professional indemnity insurance.

CHOOSING YOUR SURVEYOR

Try to find a surveyor who is skilled, independent and particular about detail. Make sure he is acceptable to your insurer. You want him to find and report the faults, and to advise you on their significance and what is needed to remedy them. Even if a broker is working for you, be cautious about accepting his recommendation of a surveyor. After all, the broker's prime motive is to get the deal to completion; that might conflict with ensuring you know all the problems. He just might suggest a surveyor he has a cosy relationship with. Get a list of several surveyors, with some suggested by independent parties. Check out your potential surveyors for qualifications and for experience with barges in particular, and for reputation if possible. Talk to at least a couple of preferred ones, to get a feel for what they will do for you and whether you are impressed by their knowledge and approach. This is also a good way to build up a relationship with your surveyor, which often helps a lot in getting a good job done and good advice. You do not have to use a native surveyor (a number of British surveyors regularly survey barges in mainland Europe).

If your surveyor is accredited to issue UK Boat Safety Certificates, you may be able to save yourself a second (safety) survey when you take the barge to Britain. It is likely that only a British surveyor will have this qualification.

WHAT'S IN A SURVEY?

You (not the vendor, broker, or anyone else) should instruct the surveyor. The surveyor will ask you to sign a contract setting out what you expect of him and he of you. Make it clear what you want him to do, and by when. Ascertain the surveyor's fee before signing and be sure to specify if you want a market valuation or an estimate of repair costs for any defects he finds (he may charge an extra fee for this). You may want to familiarise yourself with a surveying code of practice (the Yacht Designers & Surveyors Association produces one; ydsa.co.uk/other-services/types-of-survey) before the discussion.

The most important element of the survey is inspection of the hull. Usual practice is for the surveyor to check sufficient representative areas for thickness and soundness. The process should start with the hull being pressure-washed, which the buyer usually pays for. The yard will then normally have to scrape off external coatings (paint, bitumen, etc.) in small areas to make tests. This will have to be "made good" – agree with the seller who will pay for this work. The surveyor will also check inside the hull, but expect to move equipment and perhaps to do some minor dismantling for them.

Make sure the vendor is happy with all this.

There should also be an interior inspection to identify and gauge the adequacy and condition of the barge's systems. The survey will normally include an engine check, but you should not expect the surveyor to look into or comment on the engine's innards or reliability. You cannot assume that the engine is 'surveyed', you may want to get a further assessment of it from an engineer, technician or mechanic.

In some cases it may not be feasible for the surveyor to run up the engine or other systems (if the barge has been decommissioned for example). Be prepared to be flexible, while still getting as much assurance as you can.

DOING THE SURVEYING

The barge must be out of the water for the hull inspection, in a dry dock or on a tidal grid providing ready access for the surveyor to the bottom and the stern gear. Not all docks give the surveyor good working conditions. Ask your surveyor for a list of ones they recommend, or at least for their comments on one you are thinking of using.

The interior check is usually better done while the barge is afloat. (Think how difficult it is to test the engine if the propeller is not in water!) This can be a logistical difficulty, as you may want any underwater work done after the survey while the barge is still docked, so it can be a good idea for the internal check to be done first. This may mean the surveyor has to make two visits. Discuss this in advance.

A surveyor is likely to work better if not harassed. You do not need to be there to get a good result. If you really want to be on hand, ensure you do not hinder the surveyors or interrupt too often. It can be best to meet the surveyors when nearly finished so they can show you anything significant they have found.

Perhaps more important is to make sure the vendor is not there. It may be in the vendors' interest to distract your surveyor. They may be offended at the suggestion that anything is wrong with the barge or disagree with the significance of any shortcomings the surveyor finds. If the vendor insists they will not let the survey proceed without their presence, suggest that they send someone whom they trust but who is emotionally neutral in their place, with instructions simply to provide access (e.g. keys) as required and to make sure that the surveyor does not damage the vessel.

THE SURVEY REPORT

After the inspections, surveyors need time to consider their findings and to write the report. Expect this to take up to a week. Once you have read the report, the surveyors should make themselves available to discuss with you any questions it may raise. If you have chosen the right surveyors and have formed a good relationship with them, they will probably be a source of very good advice not only on how any faults might be remedied, but also as to the possible cost of this, who might best do it for you, and even on the desirability and value of the vessel. Do not forget though that you are getting an opinion based on experience, not a valuer's appraisal.

What will you see in the report? For the hull, and for each major interior aspect, there should be an overall assessment and then a detailed list of any defects found. The surveyor will usually grade these as to seriousness and urgency for remedy, often indicating which must be done right away or in the near future.

THE RESULTS OF THE SURVEY

Now we have gone through what the survey will cover, it is time to consider what conditions concerning it you might want in your purchase agreement.

It is usual to expect the vendor to make good at his expense any significant shortcomings the survey reveals which had not been made known previously, while maintaining the agreed purchase price. However, there are some provisos. The vendor will usually expect the right to cancel the contract without penalty if the work required by the survey would cost more than a stated percentage of the purchase price (typically 10%). The purchaser can, of course, agree to fund any work beyond this amount.

On the other hand, if the barge turns out not to be economically repairable, or if the vendor refuses to pay for the repairs the surveyor specifies (even within the agreed percentage), the contract should specify that you get all your deposit back and compensation.

Dealing with equipment – whether it is there, is adequate, and works properly – is fairly straightforward. Hull considerations, however, are probably less familiar to you although they are the most important.

The minimum insurable hull thickness is 3mm. But you would not want a barge that was only that thick. Your contract should normally require a minimum thickness of 4mm and this is increasingly demanded by insurers. This is usually interpreted as meaning general thickness readings of 4mm, with minor localised pitting in a few areas allowable.

The report should include a thickness map, showing measurements extended over the entire bottom and underwater sides of the barge. In the text the surveyor will usually comment on this map, and identify any suspect or downright thin areas for attention. The surveyor should also indicate any seams, rivets, dents, etc. which need repairing. Your contract should make it clear that remedying all this will be at the cost of the vendor.

But in case some areas are too thin, you need to specify how this will be fixed. The usual practice is to over-plate, i.e. to weld on a patch of new metal which will cover the entire area concerned. Many barges have such patches, and if they are done properly they are entirely acceptable. Be a little dubious if they cover very large areas, though, and ask the surveyor if they are properly fastened to the hull. A second layer of overplating is not a good idea. If the first over-plating is now thin, it and the original plating underneath should probably come off and be replaced by new plate. This can be a tricky and expensive job.

Over-plating needs to be carried out properly. If you have the work done at a reputable yard and ask your surveyor to help you commission it, results will normally be fine.

A big question is, 'How thick should the new plate be?' You might think the answer is '4mm' because that is all thickness needed. Not so. Since most of the cost of over-plating is in the welder's labour and the docking, it makes sense to go to 6mm for the extra life it will have. Try to get this into the contract. If the vendors really balk, you may get them to accept 5mm. If they refuse to go up at all, it may be worth your paying for the extra weight of steel. It is usually a good investment.

COMPLETION

You have a contract, the survey has been carried out, the required work has been commissioned at the vendor's expense, and you have arranged your financing. You are all ready to close the deal.

Here you really do need a lawyer or notary. They may already be holding your deposit. They can certainly hold the balance while the papers are processed.

They can check that all conditions of the contract have been complied with, prepare necessary forms, arrange for signatures, and file everything official.

If you are buying a barge which is on a shipping registry in a country of which you are neither a citizen nor resident, then the transfer process will normally involve de-registration of the barge. At the end of the process you should receive an official title document from the shipping registry confirming the sale and that you are the new owner, attesting that the barge is no longer on the registry and confirming the VAT status of the transaction. These are important documents of title. You are likely to have to produce them either when you enter the UK or subsequently.

With luck, everyone is smiling. Hands are shaken, a celebratory glass or two emptied. Congratulations, you have a barge. But do remember to put all your new keys and the essential papers somewhere safe before you get too jolly!

YOU'VE BOUGHT IT! NOW WHAT?

You are now a barge owner. You are now responsible for this large object floating at someone else's mooring. What are you going to do with it?

Our first answer to this question is that you should not start from here. You should take several steps before completion day, and you should start on them as soon as you are confident that the sale really is going to go through.

GETTING READY FOR OWNERSHIP

INSURANCE

As soon as the barge becomes yours, it is at your risk. Not just the risks of fire, theft, of sinking but also liability for any damage it might do to some-one else or his property if, for example, it broke loose from its moorings.

You need insurance from day one. Well before ownership day, you should have approached at least two or three insurers, giving them a description of the barge and of your plans for it, and asking for quotes. By the great day, you should have chosen your insurer, and have cover in place.

Insurers are used to this situation, and are usually helpful and flexible in setting up cover quickly and recognising that the cover may need to be adjusted before too long as, for example, work is done on the barge, it comes into commission, or it is moved to another country.

MOORING

If you have not made arrangements with the landlord of the mooring the barge is occupying on ownership day, you may find you are in trespass or subject to unwelcome charges.

In most cases, you may be able to negotiate an extension of the agreement under which the vendor was keeping the barge there. This can be helpful in giving you some time to get things better organised. However, do think about whether you actually want to keep your new possession there. The mooring may be too exposed to weather, the effects of passing traffic, or predation by the help-yourself brigade. It may be too expensive.

If you have, or want, to move the barge to another temporary location immediately you own it, you may be able to locate short-term moorings not too far away. Short-term moorings are usually not nearly so difficult to find as good long-term ones. Ask around locally, ask the vendor, ask the broker. Mooring charges may still be higher than you like (but in some areas free short-term moorings can be found), but at least you will be legal.

REGISTRATION

If the barge is registered in one country, but is sold to a national of another country, it is normal practice to de-register it. A vessel may be registered only to a national, a nationally registered company, or a resident foreigner, in most EU countries.

It may be a temptation to maintain the foreign registration by using an accommodation address in the country concerned, perhaps to avoid the costs of registering it at home. However, if your barge is shorter than 24m and you are resident in UK, it can be put on the UK Small Ship Registry (SSR) at very low cost. This produces ship's papers acceptable throughout Europe. However, the SSR is not a registry of title so cannot be used to confirm ownership or liens.

The SSR is currently operated by the UK government's Maritime and Coastguard Agency (MCA Appendix 1 for address). If your vessel is over 24m, you may register it with the British Registry of Shipping. This is not compulsory: it is a costly and lengthy business relative to the SSR. Non UK residents can register their barge on the UK Part 1 register by forming a UK limited company to own the barge. You probably do need a lawyer for this!

You will almost certainly need to register the vessel with the navigation authority for the waters you will keep it on, putting you on the authority's books for levying navigation charges etc.

FAMILIARISATION

Particularly with a sophisticated conversion, a barge is a complex object. It has a lot of systems, and quirks. It needs to be maintained and operated properly if equipment is to do what it should and to have a reasonable life. How can you avoid getting things expensively wrong when you take over?

If you can, and if they know anything, get close to the vendor or even an owner before them. Find out if they have any useful written information such as receipts, manuals, suppliers' addresses, wiring and plumbing diagrams: insist they are all given to you. Ask them to go through the barge with you in detail, explaining everything, what it does, where it is, how it works, what supplies it needs, what replacement parts should be kept on hand, what you must and must not do, how to handle any common problems. Keep asking questions until you are comfortable. Take copious notes. If the barge is mobile, ask them to go on a short cruise with you. Watch carefully, ask more questions, take more notes.

If no suitable former owner is available, try and find someone else to advise you in the same way. Your surveyor might do it (perhaps at a price), or might be able to recommend someone else. Do you have any barge-owning friends who seem to know a thing or two? If you will be having work done on the barge right away, can the boatyard owner be of any use?

The information you get is of great value to you. Treat it with respect. File it properly and safely. You might even assemble it into your personal Barge Operators Manual, which you can update as you gain knowledge or change things on board.

At the same time, start a log for the barge. This should cover not only details of your journeys, but also your equipment purchases, maintenance and repairs. Keeping a log is very worthwhile. Not only will it help you recall your cruising experiences, it will keep track of your expenditures, and is a most useful tool for trouble-shooting, by answering questions such as: Has this problem happened before? What did I do in the period just before it happened? Is this piece of equipment still under guarantee?

Apart from anything else, such documentation will make the barge easier to sell later. Remember how you wanted to see it when you were buying?

Despite all this, you are still at the bottom of a steep learning curve. Ready yourself for a string of glitches or hitches in your first year or two of ownership. Each of these will teach you something worthwhile, and you will soon be discussing batteries and toilet systems with the best of them.

SAFETY CERTIFICATION

Before you can register with the navigation authority whose waters you wish to keep your barge on, and in some cases (particularly in the UK) before you can enter its waters, the authority may insist that you get a specified safety certificate for the vessel. In Britain, this will probably be the BSS (Boat Safety Scheme). Obtaining this requires a(nother) survey, by someone accredited by the scheme. But this inspection can be done while the barge is afloat, it is not usually too expensive, and the certificate is good for four years. Principal checks cover gas and fuel systems, etc., and can result in immediate remedial work being required.

Complying with such a scheme is not an unreasonable requirement. Would you like to share a lock with a vessel with bilges full of gas?

Barges bought in mainland Europe frequently do not meet UK safety standards. The compliance work required can range from minimal (such as buying a couple of fire extinguishers) to major (re-doing all the gas piping). The rules are technical and voluminous. The usual practice in the UK is to get a preliminary inspection by a BSS surveyor so any faults noted can be dealt with before the real survey is done. However, it can be difficult to find someone familiar with the BSS rules in central France, say, although one or two barge surveyors working in mainland Europe are also familiar with BSS and might be able to give you an indication of the work needed. But if the length is over 20m overall or the length x beam x certified maximum draft in metres is over 100 then the ship will require a European Certificate (TRIWV, ES-TRIN).

ALTERATIONS OR REPAIRS

We cannot go into all the ins and outs of repairs here, but there are one or two points you might want to consider.

In many cases, the buyer moves straight from the purchase to the boatyard. There is usually some work you want to have done right away, and the survey may have revealed things that must be attended to immediately.

Underwater work (plating over thin hull spots, replacement of the stern bushing, etc.) can be done most economically while the barge is still on the slip after the survey, so it makes sense to choose a slip in a yard with a good reputation and price list for such work. That yard may also be a good choice for doing the other jobs, and you may get a lower total bill if all the work is done at the same place. However, once the barge is afloat again (and, presumably, mobile) your freedom of choice returns, so shop around.

If you have bought the barge in mainland Europe, but will be taking it to England, you have the very basic choice of whether to have the work done there or here. Many Dutch yards are very experienced in working with barges, and will readily do work that an English yard would shun. However it is harder to monitor what is going on from another country. We do not plump for either choice here, just mention that it bears consideration. You could even have the more standard work (e.g. hull repairs) done by one yard on the mainland then bring the barge to Britain for any new systems and interior refitting (which usually benefit from greater owner attention).

HANDLING YOUR NEW BARGE

All this, and you have hardly, perhaps not at all, been at the wheel yet. And if, as is not unusual, this is your first foray into barging, you may be getting a few butterflies thinking about taking charge of that metal monster which looks bigger each time you see it. Particularly if it is currently moored near some expensive plastic.
Cheer up. Most barges handle well. But, like anything else, steering them is something you have to learn. And the only way to learn it is to do it. But not necessarily on your own barge or, at least, not for the first bit.

Perhaps the pleasantest way to learn is to get invited to cruise on other people's barges. This is not necessarily the imposition you might think. Many barge skippers need crew every now and then, and may be glad of the company. Make your needs known to other owners and you may be pleasantly surprised. After all, they all had to start once, and remembering their own experiences tends to make them sympathetic.

Another option is to pay for training. There are a number of barge training schools in UK, NL and France and most advertise in Blue Flag. A few owners offer first-time steerers training on their own barges for a fee. Sometimes this simply involves going out for a few afternoons. Other operators may make it part of a holiday cruise of a week or more.

We suggested earlier that you get the vendor to take you out. This is a good way to try out your own barge with someone familiar with it on hand, and is highly recommended even for a trip of only an hour or two. Perhaps the vendor might even like to come along for a day or two on your first trip to say 'goodbye' to their old friend? It does happen, and they might be happy to be invited.

At the very least, when you move your barge for the first time, take along a couple of crew experienced in such matters. If you have not got any friends in this category, you can find someone with the right skills who will do it for a fee, and who will probably be willing to give you a steering lesson along the way. To find such a person, ask the broker, the vendor, and generally in the locality. Or contact your friendly Barge Association!

GETTING IT HOME

Bringing your new purchase home to the U.K. from darkest Belgium may be a challenge you are looking forward to. But some buyers cannot stand that much excitement, or simply may not have the time for the trip. And in any case, crossing the Channel requires special care, a long list of safety equipment (flares, pumps, etc.), and may involve substantial delay waiting for the right weather. For larger vessels, you may need crew with professional qualifications. But what do you do then if you are planning to move on board in six weeks, and you have already sold your house!

Get someone to deliver the barge for you. This service is readily available, frequently offered by people with a lot of barging experience and a good track record. Once again, inquire from the usual sources. But if you do plan to use such a service, make tentative arrangements as far in advance as possible to ensure your chosen skipper will be available when you need him.

The price for a delivery depends on the length of the trip, and whether a Channel crossing is involved. However, it is unlikely to be less than £2,000 (2022). Surprisingly, it may also be possible to have your barge brought home by truck. There are specialist haulage companies which can move vessels of 22m or even longer. Obviously a big crane is needed at each end of the journey, and sometimes even a police escort. Except perhaps for smaller barges, trucking is unlikely to be a less expensive option, but it might be a quicker one.

Before the barge sets out, be sure to check your insurance. Some insurers require an extra premium for a Channel crossing and may have other requirements such as using a properly qualified skipper.

CONCLUSION

When we first read this handbook in draft, we wondered why anyone would go through all the hassle we had documented. In fact, we wondered how we had got through it when we became owners. And it was that which made us realise that it looks much more troublesome on paper than it often proves in practice. As you pass through the process, it all tends to make sense. The advice we offer will probably seem like minor steering corrections at the time.

Despite all the potential pitfalls, the process itself can be absorbing, even fun. After all, it usually involves travelling to interesting and unfamiliar (often unsuspected) places, meeting fascinating people, and messing around in boats. Some people pay a lot of money for holidays which involve little more.

Ah yes, paying a lot of money. Well, that does come into it, of course. But if you take things cautiously and sensibly, it should prove to be money well spent. You will end up with something which, whether or not it turns out to be a sound investment in the financial sense (opinions are somewhat divided about the merits of barges in this respect), should bring enormous enjoyment into your life. And that is something you certainly can't say about everything you buy. We encourage you to try it. We would be pleased to hear how you have done.

We wish you the best of luck.

APPENDICES

Appendix 1 – Contacts

UK addresses and phone numbers nless shown otherwise.

Authorities:

Canal & River Trust First Floor
North Station House
500 Elder Gate
Milton Keynes
MK9 1BB
Tel. 0303 040 4040
www.canalrivertrust.org.uk

Environment Agency (EA) Thames Region
King's Meadow House
King's Meadow Road
Reading HRG1 8DQ
Tel. 08708 506506
www.environment-agency.gov.uk
WaterwaysThames@environment-agency.gov.uk
enquiries@environment-agency.gov.uk

Broads Authority
Yare House
62-64 Thorpe Road
Norwich
NR1 1RY
Tel. 01603 610734
www.broads-authority.gov.uk

Scottish Canals
Canal House
1 Applecross St.
Glasgow
G4 9SP
Tel. 0141 332 6936
www.scottishcanals.co.uk

Waterways Ireland
2 Sligo Road
Enniskillen
Co. Fermanagh
BT74 7JY
Tel. 0286 632 3004
www.waterwaysireland.org

Small Ships Register
Tel. 0203 908 5200
www.ukshipregister.co.uk
uksr@mcga.gov.uk

Voies Navigables de France (VNF)
175 rue Ludovic Boutleux 62400 Béthune
France
Tel. 00 33 321 632 424
www.vnf.fr

Organisations:

DBA – The Barge Association
Cormorant
Spade Oak Reach Cookham
SL6 9RQ
Tel: 0303 666 0636
www.barges.org
info@barges.org

Inland Waterways Association (IWA)
Island House Moor Road Chesham HP5 1WA
Tel: 01494783453
www.waterways.org.uk
info@waterways.org.uk

Residential Boat Owners Association (RBOA)
Studio 2
Waterside Court
Third Avenue
Burton uponTrent
Staffordshire
DE14 2WQ
Tel: 03300577180
www.rboa.org.uk

National Association of Boat Owners
NABO General Secretary
20 Oak Grove
Hertford
SG13 8AT
Tel: 07989 441674
www.nabo.org.uk
contact_us@nabo.org

Royal Yachting Association (RYA)
RYA House
Ensign Way
Hamble SO31 4Y
023 8062 400
www.rya.org.uk
cruising@rya.org.uk

Surveyors & Consulting Engineers

Institute of Marine Engineers (IMarEST)
Small Ship Group
1, Birdcage Walk
London SW1H 9JJ
02073822600
ssg@imarest.org
info@imarest.org

Yacht Brokers, Designers & Surveyors Association (YBDSA)
The Glass Works,
3b Penns Road,
Petersfield, GU32 2EW
01730710425
www.ybdsa.co.uk
info@ybdsa.co.uk

International Institute of Marine Surveying
02392385223
info@iims.org.uk

Periodicals

Waterways World (monthly magazine) 151 Station Street
Burton-on-Trent DE14 1BG Tel. 01283 742970

Blue Flag
(bi-monthly journal with many relevant barging articles)

Practical Boat Owner

Motor Boat Monthly

Appendix II – Bibliography

BOOKS

All titles are in English unless otherwise stated.
*Available to everyone from DBA - The Barge Association online
Bookshop.

* A Guide to Motor Barge Handling by E. Burrell, pub. Edward Burrell.
Techniques for manoeuvring barges, and navigating on river and canal.
Other recommended books are at barges.org/publications/books-charts

Inland Waterways of France by David Edwards-May. Comprehensive
guide providing info on locks, moorings, towns and cities etc; comes
with folding map of French inland waterways.

Cruising French Waterways by Hugh McKnight, 3rd edition, pub. Adlard
Coles Nautical, 1999. Winner of the Thomas Cook Guide Book Award:
full of information on the varied network of rivers and canals that are in
almost every region of France.

Through the French Canals by Philip Bristow, 9th edition, pub. Adlard
Coles Nautical, 1999. This book has probably tempted more people to
explore French waterways than has any other.

Through the German Waterways by Philip Bristow, pub. Adlard Coles
Nautical.

The European Waterways by Marian Martin, pub. Adlard Coles Nautical.
Manual for first-time users; regulations for cruising in Europe.
European Regulations for Inland Waterways by Marian Martin, pub.
Adlard Coles Nautical. The CEVNI rules in English.

Code Vagnon Fluvial. Regulations for cruising in France and information
for gaining PP Licence (in French).

Tests Vagnon 'Riviere' Self assessment test papers for PPL (in French).

Vagnon Carte de Plaisance. Simplified code, primarily for hirers, on French canals. (in English but not adequate by itself for PP test).

Barging About in France by T & D Murrell, pub. DBA. Booklet with guidance on cruising a barge in France; useful English/French glossary.

The Channel to the Med by Derek Bowskill, pub. Opus Book Publishing. Guide to main routes through the French canals.

Paris by Boat by David Jefferson, pub. Adlard Coles Nautical. A boatowner's guide to the Seine and Paris canals.

River Seine Cruising Guide by Derek Bowskill, pub. Kelvin Hughes. Small illustrated, full colour guide from Le Havre through Paris.

Inland Waterways of The Netherlands by Louise Busby and David Broad. Pilot guide to the inland waterways of The Netherlands for motor vessels

Watersteps through France by Bill & Laurel Cooper, pub. Adlard Coles Nautical. To the Camargue by Canal.

Watersteps round Europe by Bill & Laurel Cooper, pub. Adlard Coles Nautical. Greece to England by barge.

Back Door to Byzantium by Bill & Laurel Cooper. From the North Sea to the Black Sea.

ANWB (Dutch Tourist Board), Almanak voor Watertoerisme I and II The Dutch Barge Book by D. Evershed, pub. David Evershed Pubs. History and descriptions of Dutch sailing and motor barges 1890–1950.

Habiter une Péniche by Bernard Lécluse, pub. La Maison Fluviale, Dijon, 1996. Buying, converting and living on barges in France (in French).

Barging in Europe by Roger van Dyken, pub. Cedarbrook, Lyndon WA, 1997.

MAPS & GUIDES

European Waterways Map and Directory of European Waterways (5th edition), pub Transmanche Publications, by David Edwards-May.

Inland Waterways of France, pub. Imray Laurie Norie & Wilson. Navicartes, pub. Éditions Cartographiques Maritimes.

Inland Cruising Map of England for Larger Craft, Stanford Maritime. Ordnance Survey Guide to the Waterways, pub. Robert Nicholson.

Inland Waterways of England & Wales (map by L. Edwards), pub. Imray Laurie Norie & Wilson.

Inland Waterways map of the Netherlands pub. ANWB, Stanfords Sportschiffahrtskarten, Nautische Veröffentlichungen (Germany) ANWB (Dutch Tourist Board).

Appendix III – Inspection Check List

GENERAL
Barge name: . . . .
Vendor (name, address, phone): . . . .
Broker (name, address, phone): . . . .
Where seen: . . . .
OVERALL
Type . . . .
Sailing rig . . . .
Year built . . . .
Size
  Length . . . .
  Beam . . . .
  Draft . . . .
  Air draft (wheelhouse up) . . . .
  Air draft (wheelhouse down) . . . .
HULL
Overall condition . . . .
Exterior pitting/rust . . . .
Extent of overplating/replating . . . .
Interior protection/rust . . . .
Evidence of leaks . . . .
TOP
Shape (aesthetics, workability, efficiency) . . . .
Material . . . .
Condition . . . .
Windows . . . .
Wheelhouse . . . .
  Demountable (yes / no) . . . .
INTERIOR
Condition . . . .
Finishes . . . .
Insulation . . . .
Type . . . .
Thickness . . . .
Damp . . . .
Layout . . . .
Accommodation provided (rooms, berths) . . . .
. . . .
Headroom . . . .
Storage . . . .
Furniture . . . .

Fixed . . . .
Loose . . . .
Access for bulky items . . . .
Domestic equipment (list with type and condition of each) . . . .
. . . .
. . . .
Special features . . . .
. . . .

EQUIPMENT
Engine room . . . .
Location . . . .
Access . . . .
  For people . . . .
  From (outside / accommodation / wheelhouse) . . . .
  Type (door / hatch) . . . .
  Ease   . . . .
For equipment . . . .
  Space (headroom, crampedness) . . . .
Protection from machinery . . . .
Walls . . . .
  Fire resistance . . . .
  Insulated . . . .
Engine . . . .
  Type . . . .
  Manufacturer . . . .
  Serial number . . . .
  Year built . . . .
  Capacity . . . .
  Power . . . .
  Number of cylinders . . . .
  Maximum revolutions/minute . . . .
  Current engine hours . . . .
  Rebuild . . . .
    Year . . . .
    Engine hours . . . .
    By . . . .
    Scope of work . . . .
  Other repairs history . . . .
  Condition . . . .
  Cooling type (air, raw water, indirect, skin tank, keel) . . . .
  Exhaust . . . .
  Type (wet / dry) . . . .
  Condition . . . .

Engine instruments . . . .
  List . . . .
  Convenience . . . .
  Mounts (solid / flexible) . . . .
Fuel supply . . . .
Tanks (number; size, material, and condition of each) . . . .
  Header tank (yes / no) . . . .
  Installation and filters . . . .
Drive . . . .
  Gearbox . . . .
    Manufacturer . . . .
    Type . . . .
    Serial number . . . .
    Reduction . . . .
    Rebuild . . . .
      Year . . . .
      Engine hours . . . .
      By . . . .
      Scope of work . . . .
Other repairs history . . . .
Propeller shaft . . . .
  Diameter . . . .
  Separate thrust bearing (yes / no) . . . .
  Universal joints (yes / no) . . . .
Propeller . . . .
  Material . . . .
  Number of blades . . . .
  Diameter . . . .
  Pitch . . . .
  Condition . . . .
Bow thruster (yes / no) . . . .
  Type . . . .
  Condition . . . .
Steering . . . .
  Type (chain or cable / manual hydraulic / powered hydraulic) . . . .
  Condition . . . .
Navigation . . . .
  Lights . . . .
  Horn . . . .
  VHF radio . . . .
  Blue flag . . . .
  AIS . . . .
  Other (compass, etc.) . . . .

Safety . . . .

  Escape exits . . . .

  Ability to shed water . . . .

  Water-tight bulkheads . . . .

  Fire extinguishers (number, type, certification) . . . .

  Bilge pumps (number, location, type) . . . .

Anchors . . . .

  Number, and for each . . . .

  Type . . . .

  Winch . . . .

  Length of chain . . . .

Systems. . . . .

  Domestic water . . . .

  Tanks (number; size, materials, and condition of each) . . . .

  Pumps (number, type of each) . . . .

  Plumbing . . . .

    Material . . . .

    Installation quality . . . .

    Insulation (yes / no) . . . .

  Water heating . . . .

  Heat source (engine waste heat, generator waste heat, oil, gas, other)
. . . .

  Method (on demand or tank) . . . .

  Tank capacity . . . .

  Fixtures (list and location of each) . . . .
. . . .

Waste water. . . . .

  Toilets (list; type, and location of each) . . . .

  Disposal method(s) . . . .

Waste tanks (number; size, materials, and condition of each) . . . .
. . . .

Waste pumps (number; capacity, type, and manufacturer of each) . . . .
. . . .

Electricity

Engine DC system . . . .

  Voltage . . . .

  Battery . . . .

    Capacity . . . .

    Year installed . . . .

    Condition . . . .

    Charging methods . . . .

    Capacity of each . . . .

Domestic DC system . . . .

Voltage . . . .
Battery . . . .
Capacity . . . .
Year installed . . . .
Condition . . . .
Charging . . . .
Main engine alternator (capacity) . . . .
Charger . . . .
  Manufacturer . . . .
  Type (single stage, multi-stage, etc.) . . . .
  Capacity . . . .
Generator . . . .
  Manufacturer . . . .
  Capacity . . . .
  Cooling (air / water) . . . .
  Sound insulation . . . .
DC distribution . . . .
Parts of vessel wired . . . .
DC-powered equipment (list and details) . . . .
. . . .
Installation quality . . . .
AC system voltages . . . .
  Shore connection capacity in Amps . . . .
  Isolating Transformer and/or Galvanic isolator . . . .
  Inverter . . . .
    Manufacturer . . . .
    Capacity . . . .
    Wave form (square, modified sine, sine) . . . .
AC generator . . . .
  Manufacturer . . . .
  Capacity . . . .
  Cooling (air / water) . . . .
  Sound insulation . . . .
AC distribution . . . .
Parts of vessel wired . . . .
AC-powered equipment (list and details) . . . .
Installation quality . . . .
Heating and ventilation. . . . .
  Method, fuel and equipment for each . . . .
  Heat circulation . . . .
Ventilation . . . .
Rooms . . . .
Bilge – condition and access . . . .

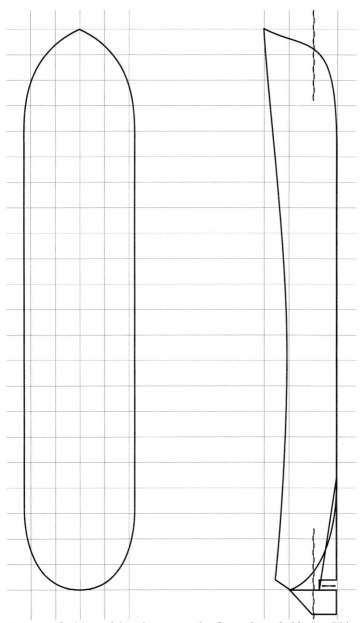

You may find it useful to draw a graph of your intended barge. This illustration, in metre squares, shows plan and elevation for a Klipper 22 m x 4.4 m. A plain graphs allows you to draw the basic dimensions of any barge. Photocopy and enlarge this blank as a first step.

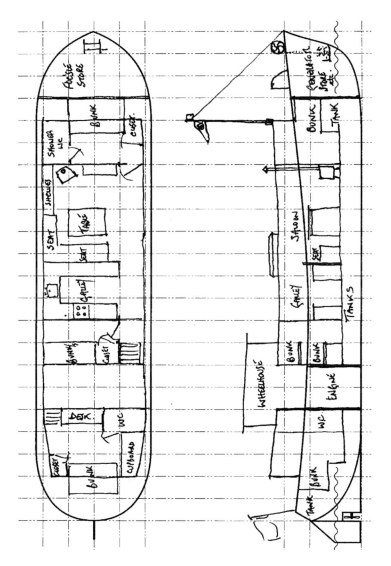

The blank can then be filled in with the basic layout with particular notes or observations you may wish to refer to later, and relate to any photographs you have taken.

YOUR NOTES

Appendix IV – Buying a Houseboat in UK

Planning to live on a static barge in England

This continues the checklist approach of the Barge Buyer's Handbook, focusing on those aspects relevant to buying a barge to be a permanent home in the UK. Life can be difficult without a permanent mooring, so much relates to the arrangements for this. Continuous cruising, ie managing without a permanent base, is possible for the smaller barge if based on the wider canals and some of the rivers, but can be problematic. Unlike the main Barge Buyer's Handbook, this document is addressed most directly to the English system, since it explores the rules and regulations and other restraints found in local legislation, but much will be directly applicable to the other UK nations.

The information in this article recognises that those looking to buy a barge to live on rather than to cruise may well carry with them the mindset of the buyer of a house or flat, especially if new to boating. You will quickly learn that boats are different. Although buying a home may be the most expensive purchase made, if that home is floating, the legal protection is minimal. Boats are regarded as chattels and the advice is Caveat Emptor, ie Buyer beware. '*This means you buy what you see and redress against the seller is limited if you later discover things are not as they seemed. Importantly the onus is on the buyer to investigate, not the seller to voluntarily disclose. However, if you ask a question, sellers are obliged to provide accurate answers or face potential consequences down the line*. So this means you need to know what questions to ask and experience shows that many advertisements for the sale of residential barges fail to provide the prompts that might be needed. There can be more safeguards with new-build barges, but they also run the same risks as second-hand barges over the mooring arrangements. When the barge is to be your home, the purchase may be taking the lion's share of your available finances, and great care is needed.

This article was based on one drawn up for non-mobile houseboats on the Thames, and has been developed in parallel with a DBA presentation for 26th April 2021 on 'Buying a barge for a static home in the UK. Caveat Emptor'. The intention is to have a living document which can continually be corrected and updated, and any feedback is most welcome. It is structured on the basis that the reader is planning to buy a barge on which to live, but much will be relevant to those who already have a barge and want to move on board permanently. The logical start is the selection of the barge, but the firm advice is this should not be considered independently of considering where it will be based. It may well prove impossible to find an acceptable mooring for that 'ideal' barge.

THE BARGE

The Barge Buyer's Handbook covers well all the important aspects of buying a barge for cruising, and if that is what you want to do, then living on board as well should be perfectly possible for extended periods. However, if the main focus is year-round living, some aspects will be particularly important. The barge needs to be suitable for all weathers including the winter months and have the storage for all your clutter. If the barge has already been modified to make a permanent home for the previous owner, be aware that this could well have compromised the ability to cruise. There are no regulations in the UK that inhibit the well-intended but bodged 'home improvement' made to what may well have started as a well-found barge.

Issues seen in barges advertised for sale as permanent homes include:

- Changes to the superstructure that increase the airdraft, from the simple prevention of the wheelhouse being able to be dismantled for low bridges to the addition of unsightly second stories that risk impairing stability as well as limiting the cruising range
- Creation of large opening windows or portholes, too-close to the waterline
- Removal of interior bulkheads to enable walk-through below decks, and other potential weakening of the basic structure of the barge
- Fitting of the interior so access to the inside of the hull is denied or made very difficult, which could be critical in particular when below the waterline
- Use of materials that are not fire-retardant including some that would not be permitted for a land-based home
- Utilities arranged so systems do not operate when no longer plugged into mains electricity or without access to water at mains pressure
- A layout as shown in publicity photos that would prove impractical with the wash found at many moorings or when cruising in non-still water

There are work-rounds for many of these, like making the electrics independent of shore supplies with a generator and inverter. But some physical changes to what might have started as a well-found vessel could be more difficult to correct and may make insurance for cruising impossibly difficult. There should be no compromises on fire safety and it needs to be recognised that there is only limited comfort from a valid certificate from the BSS (British Safety Scheme), since some important aspects are not covered or are only advisory and not compulsory. There is no requirement for BSS in some waters anyway, although aspects of gas safety apply to any vessel used primarily for domestic or residential purposes. If the barge is of a size and shape that would be acceptable at very few moorings, the purchase should be regarded as high-risk, as would the purchase of one which was not self-mobile. A pretty and well-proportioned barge may have more future options than a barge of the same length which was ungainly, say because shortened from a much larger barge.

Some barges can be rejected without expert help, but once it starts to be serious, there is no alternative to taking advice from a surveyor. He is likely to need to examine the barge out of the water. A survey is needed not just for peace of mind at the purchase but also to obtain insurance required by the navigational authority and the mooring operator. For those aspiring to cruise overseas and over 20m in length, there is merit in considering also ensuring compliance with ES-TRIN.

The arrangements for the home mooring should not be considered independent of the barge. So although this list starts with the barge, it is the home mooring that in practice is paramount.

THE MOORING: whose land and water?

Starting with those districts that would be nicest to live in and most convenient for work and schools ignores the realities of mooring supply. There are many potential barges to live on, but relatively few acceptable moorings, most particularly within commuting distance of conurbations like London. This means there is an unequal dynamic between whoever controls the mooring and those who might want to moor there. A barge that can be lived on and an official residential mooring attract a higher price together, ie this is more than the sum of the parts, sometimes very much more. The mooring is what has scarcity value, so the mooring owner holds most of the cards.

A few achieve the dream of owning their own personal freehold land alongside water where their barge can be moored: this is very difficult for newcomers and for new mooring sites there could still be insurmountable barriers with the navigational authorities and particularly the planners (see later). A small number of cooperatives have grown up where a group of boatowners have developed a residential mooring, run by a private company with the resident boatowners holding the shares. The Hermitage moorings in Wapping is one such example, a haven for mobile historic boats most of which are barges. It took several years and much capital to create. In their case, they took over an established commercial working midstream mooring with the right of land access, but other collectives have either freehold or long leaseholds on adjacent plots of land.

However, the majority of residential barges are owner-occupied on moorings which are rented. The variables are many (see table).

Table 1. Different models of the ownership of the land access - examples from Greater London			
Riparian Owner (freeholder or long leaseholder of adjacent land)	**Mooring operator. (the freeholder or on a lease from the freeholder)**	**Waters (navigation authority)**	**example**
Boat owner	Boat owner	PLA	Some at The Hollows, Brentford
Collective boatowners	Collective	PLA	Thistleworth Marine
Local Authority	Local Authority	Council	South Dock
Local Authority	charity	PLA	Chiswick Pier
Local Authority	Private company	PLA	Chelsea Yacht & Boat Co
Private Company (Tower Bridge Yacht and Boat Company Limited)	Private company	PLA, ancient rights on river bed	Tower Bridge Moorings, Bermondsey
Private Company	Boatyard	PLA	Swan Island
Crown Estate (CE)	Private company	PLA on CE river bed	Kew marine
Canal and Rivers Trust (CRT)	CRT	CRT	Little Venice
Canal and Rivers Trust	Private company (Aquavista)	CRT	Limehouse Basin
Boatowner leasehold	CRT	CRT	Benbowe Waye, Uxbridge
Private company	Private company	EA	Thames Ditton marina
Boat owner	boatowner	EA	Some at Cookham Reach
Private company	boatyard	London Medway (Peel ports)	Port Werburgh

These sorts of details behind the mooring can matter. There is very little legal protection for the barge-owner, including no freedom from harassment and no legally-enforceable security of tenure outside what is written into the mooring agreement. With moorings in such demand, mooring operators can offer 'take it or leave it' one-sided terms. Some types of operator do not have shareholders to whom they are accountable, and they may not feel susceptible to the normal decency-type restraints. There are many benign mooring owners enjoying a happy relationship with their boat residents, but all can change when someone else takes over the moorings and regards the asset as insufficiently exploited with the existing boats failing to generate maximum income. For those for whom individual or collective ownership of the mooring is just not feasible, the charitable or public sector may feel more comfortable as the landlord, at least until the pressures from austerity and COVID mean they feel obliged to sweat every available asset.

There has been a recent trend for more profit-orientated operators taking over residential moorings. Helped by generous valuations of the mooring, in particular of the intangible assets associated with planning and navigational approval, they can raise very substantial external capital from private equity. This can be a high-risk business, sensitive to changes in the housing market. Berth-holders who have paid extra capital sums for longer term 'security of tenure' could well fall way down the list of creditors were the company to fold. When due diligence on the mooring operator would be sensible, at a simple level this can be done using the Companies House beta service. This enables access to the annual accounts, although expect these to be abbreviated and minimalist and so opaque, but it should be possible to discover who is really in control, what assets have been used to secure loans, and so on. Brochures used by the mooring operator to raise additional capital may reveal plans to bring in new residential boats – maybe to the mooring you thought was yours.

As well as the variable of the type of mooring operator, there is whoever controls the waters. **Individual boat licences/registration** is required both by the Environment Agency (EA) for the non-tidal Thames and non-tidal Medway, and by the Canals & Rivers Trust (CRT) for most other non-tidal rivers, the canals and some central London docks. This licensing or registration also requires compulsory insurance of £1m (EA) or £2m (CRT) which is then a further unavoidable annual cost, even if there is no intention to cruise. On some tidal waters, however, including all Port of London (PLA) water, there is no registration system (and hence fees) for a non-commercial barge in its own right, only indirect payment through fees for the mooring.

An added dimension which matters in some places is who owns the land over which the barge is to be moored. In artificial cuts like most canals it usually falls to the CRT or whoever made the waterway. On most non-tidal rivers it belongs to whoever owns the nearest river bank, except on the non-tidal Thames below Staines it belongs to the EA. On the tidal Thames is mostly falls to the PLA, although much was unregistered until recently and some may still be. The Crown Estate owns parts of the bed of the Thames, say close to old Royal Palaces and foreshore around the coast, with sites readily identified from its own website. It is much more difficult identifying the owners of other bits of river bank, and much has remained unregistered. Once thought more a liability than an asset, there is now a drive to register river banks to facilitate action against unwelcome residential boat squatters if this were needed.

Irrespective of who owns the land under the water, the mooring infrastructure may well require approval from the navigational authority, through a River Works Licence (RWL) from the PLA, an accommodations licence from the EA, and internal approval from the CRT for those waters it controls. These approvals are the prime concern of the mooring operator rather than the barge-owner, though the cost will be passed on through the mooring fees. The fees for these can reflect whether the moored boats are used residentially.

The MOORING: the physical arrangement

Barge dwellers will need to go ashore, maybe looking smart in work clothes, or with small children or lots to carry. Getting on and off the barge needs to be easy and safe in all weathers, and possible for less able visitors too. If the water level has a potentially large rise and fall, with floods or the daily tide, then substantial built structures may be needed, say brows from the bank to a pontoon held in place with pilings, with the barge and pontoon able to rise and fall together with the water level. Some barges will be moored alongside pontoons or the quay, others alongside other barges. Some moorings dry out at low tide, maybe leaving the barge at quite a tilt. Some moorings are very susceptible to wash from passing traffic, which can create rocking movements for the moored barge, perhaps also bouncing on the bottom with certain tidal conditions. Look at the barge at its mooring at all states of the tide and ask about access in times of flood.

If there are others living immediately alongside, recognise that sound and vibrations can travel readily between hulls. Overlooking between houses is limited by regulations and the planners, but there is no equivalent for residential boats, meaning sometimes aspects of privacy may have to be sacrificed. Often there is a public right of way along the water's edge and security from those on the bank can be important. Some barges moor directly to the canal bank, whereas for others security gates have to be passed to access the boat, maybe with the added protection of CCTV.

These sorts of things may matter little for the occasional overnight stop for a cruising barge, but are of much greater importance when mooring for fulltime living. Some moorings have substantial facilities on the land, including storage and car parking and even gardens. Like higher levels of physical security, these are likely to come at a price.

THE MOORING: planning situation?

We already have the variables of type of owner of the riparian land and of the land under the mooring, which navigational authority for the water the barge sits in and the physical state of the mooring. The next on the moorings' checklist concerns the **planning position**, which falls into the responsibility of the Local Authority. This situation is complex and variable. Ignore those who say you do not need to worry about planning controls since barges aren't covered. The exemption from planning does indeed apply to a barge moored up for the night, just like a car parked on the road. They are chattels falling outside the controls of the Town & Country Planning Acts.

What can clearly fall into planning control is the mooring infrastructure, like the pontoons and pilings, though much may count as permitted development especially when undertaken by the navigational authority. If any vessel stays permanently in a location then it can lead to a change in use of the land over which it is moored, and planning approval may be needed for that. In a mixed-use mooring, like a marina or boatyard with some residential boats and some leisure ones, the proportion between the 2 can be varied to some extent, but sometimes the planners have set limits. In these mixed-use moorings, it may be necessary for the residential vessels not to have fixed moorings within the overall marina/boatyard, and some mooring operators insist on shuffling everyone around a couple of times a year to make sure this happens. 'The point at which the mooring of a residential boat on a waterway departs from an ancillary use of the waterway (which usually would not need planning permission) and moves to a material change to residential use (which usually would need planning permission) needs to be decided on the basis of fact and degree as well as the particular circumstances of the case'.

Banks of waterways are special environments: some are in conservation areas, parts may be Metropolitan Open Land (MOL), or in the Green Belt, or maybe have the path along the water's edge counting as Public

Open Space. All of these can make it problematic to get planning approval for residential use for a moored-up barge. There are increasing attempts to persuade the planners to use the public space of the main stream of the river or mainline canal only for boats in transit, and this is in various standing documents like the London Plan. Each London Borough has its own plan and there will be equivalent district plans in other parts of the country. These may make it difficult to establish completely new residential moorings, with changing existing leisure moorings to residential somewhat easier.

All this means the use of the land over which the barge is moored can be controlled by the planners, as can the mooring infrastructure, with the residential use of a boat regarded a sui generis use rather than a 'dwelling house'. The only way the vessel itself can be controlled by the planners is through conditions attached to the planning consent for the mooring. The local plan may indicate what sort of residential boat might find favour$_x$. If there are any exceptions to be permitted, this will be easier for real/traditional boats of modest size.

That's the theory of planning control, but what about the practice? A few moorings have been around so long they predate the introduction of planning controls in 1947. Many of the other older moorings may not have explicit residential consent, but they could request it through established use, which would prevent the planners taking enforcement action. This system of getting approval uses the Certificate of Lawful Existing Use or Development (CLEUD) under s191 Town and Country Planning Act 1990. All that has to be proven is that the change of use of the land, ie of the land over which the barge is moored, to residential has taken place unchallenged by the planners for the last 10 years. But it may not always be helpful to do this, and for the barge-owner there could be risks, like new controls introduced that would limit any subsequent changes to the shape and size of the vessels.

If at a mixed residential and leisure marina/boatyard there is planning approval for some residential boats, or a permit for the lawful use of only a limited number of houseboats, it may be important to check if the houseboat of interest is covered. Replies could be vague if the mooring owner is hoping to upshift the residential proportion without stimulating enforcement action from the Local Authority. There is a financial incentive for mooring owners to fudge planning approval, so try to check it out yourself. The quick way to do this is search under the postcode on the website of the local authority planning department for any past planning history and especially any enforcement actions.

With residentially-approved moorings hard to come by, what about buying a boat on an approved mooring and then just swapping it with your barge, selling on or scrapping what was there before? Is this the way to an 'official' residential mooring? Much tried and recommended in the past, approval will be needed from the navigational authority e.g. CRT will give approval if the replacement boat fits and is approved. The landlord will need to be satisfied, and is likely to want to charge more, even if no greater mooring length is required. Expect the planners to regard this as permitted development, but check for pre-existing planning restraints in either the district plan or in the specific approval for the mooring, and you may still have to argue the case. If your new barge looks good and fits in well, it should be straightforward. But if there are complaints or objections from the neighbours, it may all turn sour. There are several examples of where this has not worked out and it is unwise to assume such swaps will be nodded through without question. On those waterways where there is no requirement from the navigational authority for houseboats to be mobile or to fit in with others locally, the planning system is the only defence against unsightly floating houses. The River Thames Society, for example, advocates limits on airdraft in standing planning policies, with extra design controls on individual moorings in especially sensitive sites.

There is what is sometimes presented as a half-way house to planning approval which is **'pied-à-terre'**, an inappropriate term for a floating structure. This means the boat has approval at the mooring for occasional sleeping on board, but there is no planning approval for full-time residential use. An alternative address will have to be given which has the status as the permanent home, and the mooring agreement to be signed is likely to also indicate there can be no permanent living on board. Everyone knows that many live permanently under such arrangements, which may have advantages for the mooring operator as well as the boat resident, since it eases the way to increase the proportion of permitted lived-on vessels via the passage of time. There are risks here for the boat-dweller. After helping create a mooring approved for full-time residential use, they could find they are moved off, and if any excuse was needed, this could be from being found in breach of their mooring conditions. Other issues to consider are in box 2. This is less secure than a permanent residential mooring and if you are tempted, make sure the purchase price recognises this.

Table 2. Potential problems with permanent life under pied-à-terre mooring arrangements

- Getting a unique postal address at the barge, registering with the most local GP, generating utility bills for a new bank account, etc.

- Not paying Council Tax for local services may impact on getting children into the chosen local schools, residential parking permits, social care provision, domestic refuse disposal

- Vulnerable to enforcement action from the Council

- 'Leisure vessels' are not necessarily fit to cruise

- In breach of mooring agreement if living there full-time

- May work for you, but will you be able to sell on?

THE MOORING AGREEMENT

This is the document signed by the barge dweller with the operator of the mooring which describes the obligations on both parties and provides the main legal protection available to the barge owner. There is no standard contract in use, and it may be hard to get sight of the intended document until late in the buying process. Two of the publicly-available contracts are those used by the CRT and by Southwark Council, and it could be useful to compare those documents with what is being offered. Among the expected wording there could be conditions that might superficially sound reasonable, but are difficult to follow. For example, in parts of the tidal Thames, there seems to have developed requirements for docking after a specified number of years, even though there are insufficient docks to allow this for all the large houseboats now being moored locally. In any case, if the issue is the safety of others at the mooring, requiring third-party and wreck-raising insurance would be more logical than the process measure of frequency of docking.

Once the barge owner has broken the contract, then any supposed safeguards from having a written agreement may fall away. Some mooring operators are looking for any excuse to move boats away, since they can then either charge large sums for 'leases' on vacant moorings or else bring in boats of their own to sell at substantial profit. There is also a financial incentive for mooring owners to encourage boatowners to sell up on site, since each sale generates a substantial commission. This may not be a happy place to be for the barge resident. Box 3 includes some items in mooring agreements that might prove problematic, with top of the list the short tenure and lack of controls on future uplifts to the rent.

Table 3. Common issues seen with mooring agreements which may be a problem for you	
Limited term	At the term's end, the mooring owner can bring in someone else
No guarantee of further renewal on similar terms	Even if renewal is possible, the new terms could be excessively expensive or too onerous
No/limited maintenance permitted at the mooring	This may go beyond the sensible limiting of noise/dust to preventing even the commonest DIY.
No subletting	This may not work for you if, say, you have plans to let a family member live on the barge some of the time; may need to rent out when working overseas or when waiting to sell, or want to bring in BnB guests

Docking more frequent than required by your insurer	There may not be the available docks. The maintenance schedule should be for you and your insurers not the mooring owner to decide.
Restrictions on the barge being a place of work	This may be to fit in with the planning consent, but confirm any working from home you might need to do is also not being ruled out
No pets, drying washing on deck, use of solid fuel stoves	If these would affect the way you plan your life, you may need to look elsewhere
Limitations on subsequent sale at the mooring	Is this permitted, and if so, what cut is taken by the mooring operator? Can the new buyer expect similar terms?

The MONEY TAX

Residential boats float in a largely tax-free environment. There is no stamp duty to be paid on the barge. Barges for permanent residential use which are qualifying vessels over 15 tons should be zero-rated from VAT, as are sometimes the charges for their moorings. There should be no risk of capital gains tax: boats are regarded as chattels and so tangible moveable wasting assets and if the barge is used as the main residence, there is also private residence relief. This does mean that they also cannot be used to offset losses elsewhere. One tax that should be being paid is Council tax. The resident barge owner may be charged direct, almost always at band A, though sometimes 50% of this. Others at a collective/group mooring/marina without a promised fixed berth may be charged through the mooring fees: the costs here are shared out among all those at the mooring and payment made via business rates. If there is no direct or indirect contribution being made to Council tax, question the legitimacy of residential use at the mooring.

The MONEY – who gets paid what

There are several different parties wanting to take your money and making comparisons of the overall relative costs between different barges for sale can be difficult. There is the advertised upfront sum which goes to the seller of the boat. At the time of the sale, there may also be a percentage which goes to the mooring operator to allow the barge to be sold on rather than off the mooring, usually paid by the seller rather than the buyer but check this before you commit. The maximum usually quoted is 10%, but it can be zero, with no threshold limits. Expect to pay a regular annual mooring fee, for which the DBA should shortly have comparative data. Some mooring operators also sell 'leases' or longer-term mooring agreements for which they charge capital sums. At the period end, the options are limited to paying up again or losing the home mooring: this sort of intermittent charges for residences is not permitted for leasehold flats nor for land-based mobile homes on approved sites. Other charges may be specifically to cover unusual costs for the mooring operator, e.g. capital improvements or increased charges they are expected to bear from the navigational authority. For some moorings there may be optional extras like reserved car parking or land stores. It all adds up. On top there are the charges for registering/licensing the barge with the navigational authority for some but not all waters, docking and insurance costs which may not be optional, and also all the regular maintenance of the boat. This means there's a long list to use when comparing different barges for sale.

The MONEY – is the price right?

There is no register of prices at which barges were sold, and the advertised prices could be way off the mark. Basically, it comes down to what someone is prepared to pay, in ignorance of the actual 'market rate'. Since mortgages are hard to get and only short term and for a small proportion of the price, there is no sense check as would come from the valuation for a mortgage on a property on the land. The difficulty of persuading lenders to help with the purchase should serve as a warning that residential boat buying is insecure. Comparisons between those barges for sale being sold for residential use are confounded by so many variables, most particularly around the mooring arrangements. Experience suggests that high cost does not always mean high value. It also seems that over half the cost of a barge promoted for living in the London area may be associated with the mooring arrangement, rather than the barge, even though this is an intangible asset with any security often only very short-term.

Check other barges for sale to help estimate what proportion of the asking price is associated with the mooring arrangement. Add up all the various costs to check the overall is affordable, and try some 'what if?' contingency planning for the future. Ask around and see if your surveyor is prepared to offer advice on not just the value for cruising insurance, but for the package as a whole. You may not like an honest answer, of course. The asking price should be for the start of negotiations, and use any issues identified though this checklist to your advantage.

YOUR FUTURE

You may be living on your barge for the rest of your life, but most barge dwellers decide to move on at some stage. So it is worth thinking of your exit strategy before you commit. With a high % commission on sale going to the mooring owner, and typically a high % required by the selling/estate agent too, the barge will have to inflate in value for you not to be losing money. This is not different to the housing market more generally, but if you plan to move ashore you may find the relative prices of bricks and mortar have not changed in parallel with the prices of boats. The residential boat market can be fickle, so needing a quick sale may not work out, yet you may also find your mooring conditions prevent you renting the barge out as an interim measure whilst awaiting a better time to sell.

There could well be changes ahead for residential boats more generally. There are currently what some might regard as freedoms yet other regard as deficiencies in the formal controls in areas such as planning, the tax regime, environmental pollution and safety. Control of discharges from solid fuel heating and from diesel engines and restrictions of grey as well as black water could all be anticipated and should all be manageable with enough notice. Closing existing tax concessions would make a more substantial difference to the market. In the long term, there will be sustained changes in water levels and flow rates on rivers, for which living afloat could be part of the solution as well as being affected directly. Checking the estimates for the local flood level with the time of expiry of the mooring agreement may make paying over the odds for that very long lease not seem so wise after all.

SUMMARY CHECKLIST

The checklist in appendix III of the Barge Buyer's Handbook covers much of the detail about the barge. This was drafted on the assumption that the barge was mobile and the buyer had an interest in keeping it that way. The following tries not to duplicate that list but focuses on what seems particularly important for those wanting to buy a barge as a permanent home.

Table 4 Summary Checklist
THE BARGE [All the checks in the barge buyer's handbook, and especially/also]
Does the owner own what they are selling?
Insulation for year-round living?
Strength weakened by changes to hull or superstructure?
Has the fitting out of the interior compromised access to the bilges and hull?
Additional superstructure affecting airdraft or stability?
Adequate freeboard to any opening windows/portholes?
Fire-resistant linings, adequate exits for emergencies, fire safety?
Will enough systems still work when the barge is away from the home mooring?
If you get thrown off the mooring, could this barge fit in anywhere

else?

THE MOORING [visit at various times and if applicable, also at all states of the tide]

Is there a permanent mooring as part of the package?

Whose waters, ie which is the navigational authority?

What is the rise and fall of the water and does it drain right out at low tide?

How much wash from passing traffic? Much floating rubbish?

Barge expected to settle at a tilt when the tide's out? Is that OK with you?

Any noise from road/rail/airport/heliport/ferry etc?

What infrastructure does the mooring have and how is that maintained?

Supplies of mains power, fresh water, disposal of black water and rubbish?

What happens in times of flood?

How easy is access to the barge?	
Moored alongside and immediately adjacent to another boat? Privacy?	
What's security like from the bank?	
Any optional extras like parking and land store?	
Planning approval: [check on Local Authority planning portal]	
Does this include permanent residential use? Is there a formal limit on the number of boats lived on and where does 'your' barge fit in?	
How long have houseboats been there? If permanent residential use is not explicitly approved, has it been ruled out? Has there ever been a planning application turned down, or any enforcement action taken or threatened against houseboats? What if anything does the local plan say about houseboats?	
Is the mooring classed as leisure or pied-à-terre?	
The management of the moorings [check mooring operator website and with Companies House]	
Who's the riparian owner and their relationship with the mooring	

operator?	
Who operates the mooring and what sort of organisation are they?	
Might the mooring operator be insecure, say financially or from a short lease?	
Is there a local residents' association for like-minded boat dwellers?	
Has the mooring operator plans for or a track record of wanting to bring in his own boats to sell on the moorings, which would then need to be vacant?	
The mooring agreement [compare with other agreements, eg that for moorings run by CRT]	
What is the term of the agreement?	
What justification if any has there to be for non-renewal?	
Is it explicit how the monthly/annual fee can be changed?	
What's included and what could be extras? Utilities (like clean water and sewage)? Council Tax? Fees towards the cost of the accommodations licence or River Works Licence? Regular maintenance and cleaning of the mooring structure? Parking for bicycles or cars? Land store? Scope for one-off exceptional items to support capital works?	

What restrictions on pets, maintenance, work or paying guests on board, etc?
Potential for a tender or dinghy alongside?
What requirement for boat insurance?
Requirements for regular docking or out-of-water surveys?
Transferable to new owner? If not, how is the barge in the market for you?
If transferable to new owner, would this be on similar terms?
% commission expected on transfer at the mooring? And who pays?
Residents' association recognised? Arbitration system for any disputes?
Track record of problems at the mooring? Why is the barge owner selling up? How many others at the mooring are also on the market and why?
THE MONEY [make multiple comparisons with other barges +/- moorings on the market]
Asking price for the barge?

Any share of freehold or leasehold involved and if so, is there stamp duty to pay?	
Any capital sum also expected to the mooring operator and what does that buy?	
Annual fee for the mooring and what does that cover?	
Council tax (unless included in the mooring fee)	
Extra standing charges, eg for utilities	
Optional extras like reserved parking	
Navigational authority registration/licensing annual fee?	
Compulsory insurance costs (required for mooring or by navigational authority)	
Inescapable out of water survey to enable that insurance?	
Estimated maintenance costs of barge	
% commission you have to pay if wanting to sell the barge at the mooring?	

FINALLY

This addendum is full of warnings because of the risks for those who take the plunge to buy a barge for their home without doing adequate homework. Many of the advertisements for barges for homes appear scant with the sort of detail needed to be sure the purchase is wise, with too many being almost silent on the most important aspect, the agreement for the mooring. Makeover programmes on TV have made this worse: the focus is always the floating home with the mooring barely mentioned, if at all. When it is 'buyer beware', any purchase approached in this way can lead to disappointment or much worse, with all of life's savings at risk.

The aim is to have and be comfortable with the relevant facts, about the barge and how it can be used for a new life afloat.

This advice and checklist is drafted in good faith by a non-expert with no commercial interests in buying and selling of barges and without any claims to be authoritative, aiming to help a barge purchaser make a decision which works best for them.

Good luck. If not already a member of the DBA, please join.
Hilary Pereira ©DBA 2021

ABOUT DBA

The aims of DBA are to:
Promote interest in barging
Be the representative body for non-commercial barging
Be the premier source of barging information
Establish contact with and influence other relevant clubs, societies, navigation authorities and trade associations.
Keep members informed on all barge related topics
Facilitate communication between members to provide the opportunity for discussion of all aspects of barging.

Membership of DBA offers you these benefits:

Blue Flag: DBA's colour magazine, sent to members bi-monthly.
Events: Rallies and social occasions are held throughout the year.
Forum: Discussion between members accessible either online or by email
www.barges.org/forum/index
Waterways Guide: Information from members about moorings and services on the waterways.
Knowledgebase: A compendium of information from members via Blue Flag, the Forum and other research.
DBA Shop: Books & burgees are available.
Members Discounts: Various suppliers have agreed to give discounts to DBA members.

For further information contact the membership secretary:
www.barges.org
membership@barges.org
0044 (0)3036 660636

Cambrian Printers Ltd Llanbadarn Road Aberystwyth Ceredigion SY23 3TN 08T
United Kingdom

ISBN 978-1-7397437-0-3

END